assachuset   *1's*
vorce Han

by attorney Isabella Jancourtz

ISBN 0-9618632-3-4

i

UNCONTESTED DIVORCE FORMS

CONTESTED DIVORCE FORMS

CONTEMPT FORMS

"209A" PROTECTION FROM ABUSE FORMS

MODIFICATION FORMS

COMPLAINT FOR GRANDPARENTS VISITATION

Introduction

This book is intended to demystify the legal process you will experience if you decide to end your marriage.

It is no substitute for a lawyer, but if you have a lawyer it will help you understand her or his activities on your behalf. If will also tell you how to go about finding a lawyer and whether or not you need one.

If you are representing yourself, this book will help you find your way through the Massachusetts Probate and Family Courts.

The past few years have brought numerous changes in the law of divorce. In some ways getting a divorce has become easier.

Increasingly people are choosing to represent themselves, although they may also occasionally consult with an attorney. The courts are responding to pro se litigants by offering some written information. In many courts, there is a volunteer **lawyer of the day** who is available to answer questions and provide assistance in filling out forms.

The **Family Service Office** in each court provides trained mediators who attempt to help litigants (whether or not represented by lawyers) resolve financial and other disputes prior to arguing motions or other pleadings before a judge. Many times all or most of the issues are resolved in mediation, and the family service officer or one of the attorneys drafts a **Stipulation** which all parties sign.

The **child support guidelines** have been in effect since 1987 and were amended again in 1997, this time to provide a 50% credit for the cost of medical insurance, regardless of which parent pays it. Previously the credit was only available to the parent paying child support. The guidelines have been invaluable in establishing automatic and adequate amounts of child support. You will have to do little more than show up in court with your own financial statement, after making proper service upon your husband, to obtain child support pursuant to the guidelines.

Child support and **education expenses** may now be awarded up to **age 23** for dependent children who are full-time students.

Mandatory income assignment creates an absolute right to a wage or pension deduction for child support or alimony. Most support orders are now made by **wage assignment,** greatly reducing the incidence of unpaid support.

The 30-day living apart requirement has been abolished. It is now possible to file for divorce even though you and your husband may still be sharing the same home.

An identifying witness is also no longer necessary. A constable or sheriff alone can make service of the divorce complaint and summons.

The **Abuse Prevention Act** allows the filing of a **"209A" complaint** in probate or in district court and issuance of emergency temporary restraining and vacate orders. It has resulted in a greater degree of sensitivity to and protection for battered women by the courts and the police.

There have been significant amendments to Rule 401 on **financial statements** as of December 1, 1997 There is an 8 page form required for those with gross annual incomes of $75,000 or more. Those earning less than $75,000 file a 2 page financial statement. Now attorneys must also sign financial statements to affirm that they have no knowledge of any false information.

There must be an exchange of financial statements within 45 days of the service of the divorce complaint and summons or within 2 business days of a hearing, if scheduled sooner. A formal demand may be made for an updated financial statement upon 10 days notice. Sanctions for failure to comply are mandatory, except for good cause shown.

Also in effect as of December 1, 1997 is the new Rule 410 on **mandatory self-disclosure**, which requires an exchange of tax returns and numerous related documents within 45 days of service of the complaint and summons, except as otherwise agreed by the parties or ordered by the court. The entire text of this important new rule is reprinted in the Appendix. It may make additional discovery unnecessary, resulting in a great savings of time and money.

Another important new rule is Rule 409 on **Case Management.** See the Appendix for the entire text of this rule, which provides a conferencing process that could save a great deal of time, money and aggravation.

Also new to probate practice as of December 1, 1997 is Rule 56 **Summary Judgment** which can be used in actions for modification and actions to modify or enforce a foreign judgment. This will considerably lessen the time needed to dispose of certain "cut and dried" matters, such as the application of the child support guidelines in actions to modify child support.

There have also been some recent changes in the rules regarding **motions.** It is now necessary to provide a **proposed order** for each motion, namely a statement of the exact order you wish the judge to make. It is also necessary to provide more notice for a hearing on a motion: 10 days if by mail and 7 days if personal service of the motion is made.

Parenting courses are now required in Berkshire, Franklin, Hampshire, Hampden, Norfolk, Plymouth and Worcester counties, when there are minor children.

The Supreme Judicial Court's 1989 **Gender Bias Study** determined that bias against women pervades the court system, damaging the quality of justice citizens receive in Massachusetts courts. The Gender Bias Study Committee found that "although male attorneys emerged in our research as the worst offenders, we must also recognize the part that court employees play in making the courthouse environment an uncomfortable and sometimes hostile place for women."

The Gender Bias Study Committee found three recurring problems in the family law system. 1 Women litigants lack access to adequate legal representation. 2 Financial statements submitted to the courts are inaccurate in many cases, and the courts fail to take seriously the rules surrounding discovery in family law cases. 3 Mediation, used extensivly in the courts in family law cases, presupposes litigants are on an equal level, when, in fact, women may actually have greater economic risks and less information about their assets and legal rights than men.

Some of the recommendations in the area of family law are: 1 stricter financial statement requirements and penalties for failure to disclose income and assets, including pension and other deferred compensation, 2 relief of pressure, both on family service officers and litigants, to rush settlements in court, 3 sensitizing court staff to signs of unequal power in the dynamics between the parties, unfair concessions, and the effects of abuse on the parties and on the children whose custodial parent is being abused, 4 amendment of Massachusetts General Laws, chapter 208 section 34 to include among the factors a judge must consider, lost career opportunities on the part of the wife, and the tax consequences of financial settlements, and 5 more assistance for women who represent themselves in spousal abuse cases.

Although some progress has been made in the nine years since the **Gender Bias Study** was completed, most of the recommendations have not yet been implemented, in part due to lack of funds. One very significant response is that courts now order lawyers fees at the beginning of a divorce action.

This book is written especially for women going through divorce in Massachusetts, although men have also found it useful since it was first published in 1974. It is always interesting to hear from my readers, whose questions and comments have taught me a lot.

Divorce is inevitably tough on the whole family, but the problems of women and children are almost always the most severe. The courts rarely, if ever, see a battered man seeking protective orders, or a father and children who are being evicted from their home, or can't afford to eat, because the mother has stopped paying support.

Hopefully, this book will help you understand and survive the process of divorce, minimize the impact of the inequities which still exist, and reach a resolution that everyone can accept and then live with.

It must be emphasized that this handbook is only an outline of divorce law and practice in Massachusetts. It cannot replace the advice and assistance of a competent attorney. Good legal representation is recommended in all but the simplest uncontested cases, those which do not involve children or property. If at all possible, you should have at least one meeting with a lawyer before you take any action described in this book.

June 8, 1998   Isabella Jancourtz
P.O. Box 743
Weston, Massachusetts 02493

Chapter 1   THE DECISION TO DIVORCE

People getting married these days are aware that the statistics give them a 50% chance of staying together. Divorce has become a major phenomenon of our time. Because of the high incidence of divorce and its wide acceptance by society, some see it as the only solution to a marriage that is not working.

Divorce, however, can create many more problems than it solves, especially when there are children. Like the decision to marry in haste, the rash decision to divorce is often regretted.

Sometimes it is the attitude, and not the situation, that needs adjustment. A marriage that is not working needs more and better communication. Outside help, such as counseling, may be required. Time apart may be needed to give each person a rest. Possibly getting away together is the answer for you. Groups like Marriage Encounter have saved many floundering marriages, and their key is said to be opening up the lines of communication.

Courtesy, consideration, and kindness are contagious. It is never too late in a marriage to give and get respect, but you do have to give it to get it. It is possible to transform a bad marriage into a good one by treating your spouse as you would like to be treated.

None of us is perfect. Without forgiveness, no marriage can survive for long. To forgive is what all religions teach us to do. Of course, there are limits, things that are difficult, if not impossible, to accept or tolerate, such as physical abuse. It is against the law, and you can get help.

We are living in difficult and stressful times. Age old values have been discarded by many as too confining. Commitment, loyalty, and real unconditional love are hard to find. Small wonder so many marriages are falling apart.

Boredom accounts for many divorces. So do adultery, alcoholism and abuse of all sorts. Many marriages are eroded by arguments over money, lifestyles, sex, in-laws, and children. Lack of communication is the reason most often given by people seeking to end their marriages.

Major changes, like the birth of a child, sickness or divorce in the family, death, unemployment, or other loss, raise the level of tension between a couple. An angry outburst can cause a rift that nobody wanted.

Some time ago, a woman who came to see me explained that her decision to divorce was made while putting, or trying to put, her young child to bed. The child was crying, wanting attention, and an argument erupted between the parents as to whether or not one of them could respond. One parent yelled, "Don't go in there. Let him cry." The other parent stormed in anyway shouting, "Don't try to tell me what to do." By the time the child got to sleep that night, each parent had declared they wished the other dead, and the marriage had sputtered to its senseless conclusion. This mother and father could have instead apologized to one another for the scene, and then sat down and communicated about their different ways of caring for their child. A family therapist could have been consulted.

1

How unspeakably tragic are the moments of marital breakdown. A dream has been shattered, a partnership ended. Yet when the moment is happening, wife and husband are too involved with their own hurt, angry feelings to see or appreciate the big picture. Many people realize too late that they made the wrong move when they decided to part. Think about it. Is divorce really right for you? What about your family?

If there is a shadow of doubt and/or a glimmer of hope in your mind, do the sensible thing and find a therapist or a marriage counselor pronto. He or she can help you figure out what's happening, what you need, and what the realistic expectations are. Forget your passion for privacy, your pride, your busy schedule, your pocketbook. Saving your marriage is worth it. Insurance may cover most of the expense. Go alone at first if you have to. Your counselor may succeed in getting your husband to come to future meetings.

Of course, you are the best judge of whether any given therapist or counselor is the right one for you. Don't hesitate to change if the relationship feels wrong. However, be honest with yourself. Don't quit your counselor just because you are not thrilled with what you are finding out about yourself, your marriage, and the way your family operates. After all, you are there because things are NOT working well, and you have to face the tough issues and work through them before things can get better. Most women's centers give referrals to reputable therapists and counselors.

A marriage in trouble needs help fast. Friends and family are hopefully there for you, but their bias in your favor may work against you. Well-meaning people telling you how right you are can ruin your perspective on the situation. A professional counselor, or a spiritual advisor, can help you to see things straight.

Sometimes joining a group of people in the same boat is a good idea. No one can understand what you are going through as well as someone who has been through it. That is why groups like AA and Al-Anon are so successful. Many groups have workshops for people who are going through divorce, or thinking about it.

The decision to divorce or to stay married is yours to make. It is also yours to live with. Give yourself enough time to think about it clearly before you act.

If the decision to divorce has been made for you by your spouse, you may be in a state of shock for several weeks or months. A good counselor can help you pull yourself back together. It is important that you see a lawyer as soon as possible, even if you don't really want to, and especially if your husband insists that it isn't necessary.

There are numerous divorce support groups in the area, offering advice, information and moral support. For listings of meeting times and places, check the Boston Globe **Calendar** section published on Thursdays, or your local paper.

Chapter 2   THE ALTERNATIVES TO DIVORCE

It is rarely a good idea to dash off to court to file a complaint for divorce without first considering the alternatives. Once a divorce complaint has been filed, you may lose other, possibly better, options that were formerly available.

Reconciliation

Filing a complaint for divorce is a clear message to your spouse that the marriage is over. It is not a good idea to file while you are in the heat of passion, "just to show him" how hurt or angry you are, if what you really want is to eventually make up. Chances are that he will take up the idea of divorce and refuse to consider any later talk of reconciliation.

First, allow your emotions to cool down somewhat, and then stop and think whether ending the marriage is what you really want. If what you want is for things to be different, then communicate this to your spouse.

You may be so confused that you don't know what you want. Try talking to a trusted friend, a professional counselor, or a pastor, priest or rabbi. Sometimes writing things down helps to sort them out in your mind. Getting away for a day or two may give you the perspective you need.

There certainly are couples who manage to reconcile during or even after divorce, but they are the exception. For most people, the filing of a divorce complaint signifies the end of a marriage, rather than a new beginning. Think seriously about whether the marriage can be saved before, rather than after, you file for divorce.

Every marriage has its rocky moments, and many formerly married people have regretted the hasty decision to divorce. Once a complaint for divorce is filed, it becomes much more difficult to reconcile. Some lawyers make an effort to determine first off whether a reconciliation is possible. Many do not, and for that reason, a good place to start considering divorce and the alternatives is with a counselor or therapist.

Marriage Counseling

Marriage counseling is a process whereby husband and wife attempt to understand and resolve their differences. Sometimes the goal is reconciliation. Sometimes the goal is a civilized separation. Most of the time one or both partners is unsure of the future of the relationship. The marriage counselor helps to re-establish or improve communication between husband and wife.

Because of fear, pride, and other reasons, some men who love their wives refuse to go to marriage counseling. You should consider going alone, especially if you are confused about what to do. Some counselors are quite good at calling and persuading hesitant husbands to come in for a session. Most men go to counseling once they realize it is the only hope for continuing the marriage. A judge can order counseling upon request of one party.

3

The counselor should be trained and experienced in helping married persons talk constructively about their problems. The counselor should not take sides, but be neutral and give both partners equal time to air their grievances. The counselor may want to see each of you individually at first, to get each person's side of the story without interference from the other.

Be honest about your problems, your wishes, and intentions. Let your counselor and your spouse know if and when your goals change. As with attorneys, not all counselors are competent, and you should form your own opinion as to whether you are being helped. Try to get a recommendation from a person or group you trust.

Family Abuse Prevention

If the problem is violence, relief may be obtained by filing a complaint under the **Abuse Prevention Act**, Massachusetts General Laws, Chapter 209A. This is the procedure to use for emergencies in which you require immediate protection from serious physical harm. Most abuse prevention claims are filed in the **district courts**, because they are local and therefor more convenient for the parties and for the police, who may appear as witnesses. However, **209A complaints** may also be filed in **probate court.**

You should go in person to your local **district court** or to the **probate court** for your county. You will not need a lawyer. The clerk will help you fill out the 209A complaint. There is no filing fee. There is no need to file a complaint for divorce. See the Appendix for lists of probate and district courts and a sample 209A complaint.

When you are called before the judge or hearing officer, describe the events or threats that cause you to fear for your own or your children's safety. The judge will give you temporary vacate and restraining orders, requiring your husband to leave the house and to leave you alone. If you have children, you may also receive a temporary custody order at the first hearing.

At night and on weekends, your local police will call an available judge for you, to issue emergency protective orders. You must then go to court on the next business day to file your 209A complaint. When you file your complaint and receive your emergency protective orders, you will be notified of the date when you must return to court. The police will serve the complaint and summons on your husband, notifying him of the emergency protective orders, and of the hearing date. The hearing generally takes place within five days of the day you file your complaint.

At the second hearing, both you and your husband will be questioned by the judge concerning the family violence problem. If the judge is convinced that violence has been or may be a problem, vacate and restraining orders may be issued for up to a year, and renewed as needed after that.

The district court judge may also issue temporary orders for custody and for payment of support. These orders remain in effect until further action is taken by the court. In the event you decide later that you want a divorce,

4

you must go to the probate court and file a divorce complaint. The support and custody orders issued by the probate court will supersede the prior orders of the district court.

If you are afraid to go to court alone, bring a friend or call your local women's center. Many women's centers have support groups for battered women, including trained volunteers who go to the district court with you.

For your safety, you may wish to move to a new address and not let your husband know where you are. If you request it, the court will **impound** your address, keeping it confidential from your husband and his attorney.

Call the police immediately if your husband violates the vacate and restraining orders. They will remove him from your home and, if necessary, put him in protective custody or arrest him. Violation of the vacate and restraining orders is a criminal offense and can result in a fine of up to $5,000 or sentence to prison for up to 2½ years.

Living Apart With a Written Agreement

If you and your husband decide to separate for more than a few weeks, it is a good idea to try to reach agreement on your finances and property. If you have minor children, you will also want to discuss and agree on living arrangements, visit schedules, support, insurance, and other issues.

Whatever you agree to orally should be put in writing to avoid confusion, disagreement, and possible litigation later. The best approach is for each of you to see a lawyer **before** making any written agreement. Generally, one attorney will draft a proposed agreement, and the other attorney will review it. If you and your husband have agreed on the major issues, the lawyer's fee for drafting the agreement will be relatively inexpensive.

The agreement goes into effect once it has been signed by both of you. Chapter 7 describes the provisions generally included in a separation agreement. Most agreements made by husbands and wives living apart are designed to remain in effect in the event of a subsequent divorce. Some are designed to be temporary, and these are limited in scope, for example, stipulating only the amount of support to be paid during a marital separation.

The obvious benefit of living apart with an agreement is that your differences are settled. Peace can be expected to prevail. Both parties can feel relatively secure with an agreement in writing. If there is a breach, the agreement is enforceable in court.

Some people fear making a separation agreement will spoil their chances of a reconciliation, and prefer to leave everything up in the air until it is resolved whether they will stay together or not.

One consideration is that as time goes by, the chances for reaching a good or fair agreement may diminish. As the adulterous husband's guilt subsides, for example, so does his offer of a decent settlement. The middle-aged wanderer exclaiming, "Take the house. Take the car. Take everything! Just give me my freedom!" on July 4, should be asked to immediately convey title to the house and car, and to put the entire agreement in writing. The same spouse may be feeling considerably less generous come September.

A written separation agreement between husband and wife allows for a separation with fewer snags, and insures that any subsequent divorce will be uncontested. Moreover, a separation agreement does not generally interfere with the chance for marital reconciliation, as does the filing of a complaint for divorce. If properly drafted and executed, it is a valid contract, binding on both parties, without any court action whatsoever.

Living Apart Without a Written Agreement

If you have a reasonable oral agreement regarding care of the children, finances, etc., you may not want to bother making a written agreement. This is especially true if you see your separation as temporary, maybe a cooling off period after an awful fight, or great disappointment.

This is fine on a short-term basis for most couples, and is, in fact, common among newly separated couples. However, if the separation lasts for more than a few months, it is generally best to put your agreement in writing. The danger is that as time goes by, there may be a change of heart, or an honest confusion, about what was agreed to.

Judgment of Separate Support

A judgment of separate support issued by a probate court gives you the legal right to live apart from your husband, and makes provisions for child custody, child support, alimony, division of property, and visitation. It does not, however, end your marriage. A **complaint for separate support** is used rarely, generally by people who have decided that they will live apart but never divorce, perhaps for religious reasons.

The **grounds** for separate support are (1) failure to provide suitable support without justifiable cause, (2) desertion, (3) living apart for justifiable cause, and (4) justifiable cause to live apart, although the parties may still be living together. "Justifiable cause for living apart" can be almost any serious reason.

Your husband may attempt to contest your separate support complaint by asserting the defense of condonation, or forgiveness on your part, or by denying that he has failed to support you or deserted you, or that there is justifiable cause for you to live apart from him.

The procedure for separate support is similar to that for divorce, with some important exceptions. (1) There is no 30 day living apart requirement. (2) There is a $61.00 filing fee. (3) Your husband must receive **actual** notice. He must be served a copy of the separate support complaint and summons by a sheriff or constable, or by a disinterested party. Your husband may also accept service by signing the summons in the presence of a notary public. (4) All the provisions of the separate support judgment are effective immediately. There is no waiting period.

6

You can get **temporary orders** in the same manner as with a complaint for divorce, and you can return to court for modification of the orders as needed. All of the protections available in divorce, such as **mandatory wage assignment, vacate** and **restraining orders** are also available in separate support actions.

At some point after you have obtained a judgment of separate support, you may wish to end your marriage by getting a divorce. You will have to file a complaint for divorce, going through a whole new court proceeding.

Annulment

An annulment is a judgment which declares that you were never legally married. You can get an annulment if one of the following situations apply to you.

Mental Incapacity You or your husband were insane or feebleminded, in the custody of the department of mental health, or committed to an institution at the time of the ceremony.

Bigamy or Polygamy One of you was still married to someone else at the time of the ceremony. There is a narrow exception. If at the time you were married, you did not know that your husband already had a wife, and you continued to live with him after he divorced her, then your marriage is valid.

Consanguinity You and your husband were too closely related by blood: he is your grandfather, father, uncle, brother, nephew, son, or grandson.

Affinity You and your husband were too closely related by marriage: he is your step-grandfather, grandfather-in-law, step-father, father-in-law, step-son, son-in-law, step-grandson, or grandson-in-law.

Fraud Your husband induced you to marry him by an intentional deception. For example, he is an alien who concealed the fact that he married you only so he could remain in the United States. It is necessary that you leave your husband and seek an annulment as soon as you discover the fraud.

Duress Your husband forced you to marry him by threats of bodily harm. As with fraud, it is necessary that you leave your husband and file a complaint for annulment as soon as you are able. If your marriage has been a long one, it will generally be impossible to prove fraud or duress.

Insufficient Age Your marriage is not valid if you or your husband were under age 18 when you married, and did not have the written consent of your parents or a probate court order. To do this, you would have had to marry in another state or lie about your age.

Sham Ceremony If you and your husband knowingly refused to comply with the legal requirements for marriage in Massachusetts, including filing a notice of intention with the town clerk 3 days in advance and obtaining a blood test and marriage license, or you knowingly engaged to perform the marriage ceremony a person who was not authorized, to perform marriage, then you are not legally married. However, if you and your husband consummate your marriage in the belief that the ceremony was lawful, the lack of authority of the person marrying you or an omission of or error in the notice of intention will not invalidate your marriage.

Unlike some states which consider a couple married if they lived together openly as husband and wife, Massachusetts is not a common law marriage state.

The procedures for obtaining an annulment are similar to those for a divorce. A complaint is filed with the court, which issues a summons to be served on your husband. The filing fee is $111.00, and a certified copy of the marriage record must be filed.

If you have obtained a divorce or a separate support judgment, the court has already made a finding that there was a valid marriage and you cannot sue for annulment.

If your marriage is annulled, the court may still make an order for **child support**, just as in divorce. The **Child Support Guidelines** will apply. They are explained in the Appendix.

It is often preferable to get a divorce rather than an annulment, especially if you have children. The law considers your children illegitimate if the reason for the annulment is that you were too closely related by blood or marriage, or knowingly committed bigamy. In most other instances, an annulment will not result in illegitimacy of the children.

The concept of illegitimacy has fortunately lost its significance in many areas. It is still important, however, as far as inheritance is concerned. If for example, the children are considered illegitimate as to their father who dies without leaving a will, they are not entitled to a share of his estate as they would be if they were considered legitimate.

Although it is not possible to disinherit a spouse (see Chapter 12), it is possible in Massachusetts to disinherit a child if the will states that provision for the child was deliberately omitted.

Religious Dissolution of Marriage

An annulment in the Roman Catholic Church, a divorce pursuant to the laws of the Jewish faith, or any other religious dissolution of marriage is an entirely separate proceeding which has no effect on your legal status.

Chapter 3   REPRESENTING YOURSELF

More and more, people are chosing to represent themselves in court.   In
Boston, the Suffolk Probate and Family Court now gives out **Ten Suggestions If
You Represent Yourself in Court.**   See the Appendix for a reprint of this very
helpful little booklet, written by the Boston Bar Association.

Generally, it is easy to represent yourself in an uncontested divorce,
but not when there will be a contest.   If the parting with your husband is
reasonably friendly, you have no children, and you have no disputes over
property or support, then you are an ideal candidate of a **pro se** (appearing
for oneself, without a lawyer) divorce, with an agreeement.

If, on the other hand, your husband is abusive or irresponsible, or if
agreement is impossible, then you are generally better off with a lawyer.
Unfortunately, some lawyers are irresponsible themselves, and can make matters
worse.   It is the fate of too many women going through divorce to be exploited
financially by do-nothing or otherwise incompetent lawyers.

If you cannot afford legal fees, you may be eligible for legal aid.   See
the Appendix for a list of legal aid offices in Massachusetts.   If you do not
qualify for legal aid, you may succeed in finding a lawyer with a sliding fee
scale, or even one who is willing to work for free, or **pro bono.**   Call your
local women's center, legal aid office, bar association, or the Massachusetts
Bar Association at (617) 338-0500 for a referral.

If you wish to or must represent yourself, this book will help.   However,
if you possibly can, see a lawyer for at least one hour's consultation about
your case.   Many attorneys will not charge for the first consultation.   You
might want to hire a lawyer for an hour or two to help you draft some of the
papers you will need, or review the documents you have received.   This will
help you gain the information and confidence to handle your case effectively.

You have a constitutional right to represent yourself in any legal
matter.   Judges and clerks are not, however, required to explain the law to
you or to advise you in any way, although many do try to be helpful.   The risk
you take when you represent yourself is that your lack of knowledge of the law
will be a serious disadvantage.

If you have the time, you can minimize this risk by learning as much as
possible on your own.   Law libraries, located in court houses, in law schools,
and in some public libraries are a good place to start.   You can research the
statutes and cases that apply to your situation.   You can read detailed books
on divorce that are written for lawyers, as well as articles in legal journals
and encyclopedias.

Attorney Michael L. Leshin has written a very comprehensive work called
The Massachusetts Family Law Sourcebook.   It contains all relevant statutes,
rules and regulations and is available for $50 from Massachusetts Continuing
Legal Education, Inc., Ten Winter Place, Boston MA 02108, telephone 1-800-
966-6253.   M.C.L.E. is just around the corner from Park Street Station, next
door to Locke Ober.   You may visit its bookstore to browse through and to
purchase this and other very helpful books.

You may learn from talking with people who have been through divorce in Massachusetts recently. You can find out a lot for free or very inexpensively at workshops and lectures on separation and divorce. The Boston Globe **Calendar** section published on Thursdays, or your local newspaper has listings of these events.

Your public library is a good source of popular books and articles on divorce. Look at those written most recently first, as the law is constantly changing. Also, it is important to remember that laws vary somewhat from state to state.

Unless they have been **impounded** (made unavailable to the public) divorce records are public records and you are free to read them and learn. The Registry of Probate is where the divorce records are kept. Look in the most recent Divorce Docket Book. It lists names and docket numbers of recent divorce cases, along with the name and date of each pleading or order. Request the files you want by docket number. In this way, you can easily look up several pleadings similar to the one you need to draft.

Another way to prepare yourself is to actually sit in on some hearings in Probate Court. A courtroom is a public place and you have a right to be there, unless the matter is in rare **closed session**. A court officer may come to you and ask you your business in court, to satisfy his or the judge's curiosity, to determine how many cases are left to be heard, and/or to check out whether you are a security risk. It is okay to say that you are there to observe and to learn. Sit as close to the judge as possible so you can hear. You cannot sit inside the bar which is just for lawyers. You will probably not be allowed to read, except for legal documents, or to talk.

If you do have to go into court without a lawyer, especially if the matter is contested, bring a friend or two for moral support. If your friend is familiar with the situation, she or he may also be able to testify in your behalf.

Be sure to put every significant fact about your case in writing, otherwise you cannot count on it coming to the attention of the judge or being part of the record of your case, for future reference. It is best to put all relevant information in your motion, affidavit, or memorandum. Otherwise, you may forget or not have the time (especially in a hearing on temporary orders) to mention your very important fact.

When your case is called, walk up to and stand directly in front of the judge. You will be asked to raise your right hand and swear to tell the truth. If you are the **moving party** (the person who brought the matter to court by, for example, filing a motion), you speak first. State your case clearly and loud enough for the judge to hear. Stick to the facts and get to the point. It will help to jot down some notes about what you want to say ahead of time.

Then your husband or his lawyer will respond. Do not interrupt to disagree, but take notes of what you want to say in response or in **rebuttal**. In a hearing on temporary orders, you will only have a few minutes to talk before the judge decides that he or she has heard enough to make an order.

In a final hearing, you will have all the time you need to ask and to state the relevant facts, but you will not be allowed to ramble pointlessly, or bring up immaterial or irrelevant facts. Only the judge is allowed to draw conclusions, and you should try to avoid statements that sound like conclusions or judgments.

If you are surprised by information introduced by your husband, you can request a **continuance** of the hearing, so that you can return to court another day with new evidence or witnesses. You may also request permission to file a **memorandum** within a few days of the hearing. A memorandum is a written statement of facts relevant to your case. You may attach exhibits, such as a letter from a doctor, or a pay stub, to **corroborate** (back up) your statements. It is best to have a written memorandum ready to give to the judge at the hearing.

The judge may encourage you to get a lawyer, and suggest that you return to court with one in a few days. However, it is your choice whether you will represent yourself or hire a lawyer to do the job.

When the judge has heard all the testimony, she or he will either state the terms of the order immediately, or will decide to send the order later saying, "I'll take the matter under advisement." Either way, the mail will bring the judge's decision in a few days on a temporary order, a few weeks on a final judgment.

Be sure to keep a complete file on your case. You won't be overwhelmed by the paperwork if you keep everything in chronological order. You might get a loose-leaf notebook and make separate sections for correspondence, notes, papers filed in court (**pleadings**), court orders, and financial statements. You can number each item and make a list, or index, for easy reference.

Remember that the law of divorce is constantly changing. New statutes and new cases vary the way things are done. This is yet another reason why it is a good idea to have at least one consultation about your case with a family lawyer, even if you have decided that you want to represent yourself.

If you hire an attorney to review the separation agreement and other divorce papers, for example, you minimize the risk that the judge will find fault with and not approve your agreement. You will be less likely to make mistakes that get by the judge but come back to haunt you later.

Most judges make every effort to be courteous and fair to all who appear before them. Some, unfortunately, do not.

You may report incidents of judicial misconduct to the Judicial Conduct Commission at 14 Beacon Street, Suite 102, Boston MA 02108. The telephone number is (617) 725-8050.

The judge will be required to respond to your complaint and to account for his or her actions. You have one year from the date of the incident to file your complaint.

Chapter 4   CHOOSING THE RIGHT LAWYER FOR YOU: WHAT TO LOOK FOR

If you decide to get a lawyer, you will need one who is competent, accessible, and who charges a reasonable fee. A personal recommendation from a friend or a professional may lead you to such an attorney.

In the event no one you know can suggest a good family lawyer, you may call your local women's center for a referral. Centers for women, such as those in Chapter 14, are generally knowledgeable about local lawyers.   Most keep referral lists, and record the feedback they get about the quality of the lawyers' work. You may also call your local bar association for a referral to a lawyer in your area or The Massachusetts Bar Association Lawyer Referral Service, (617) 542-9103, or (800) 392-6164. You may request an attorney who will work for free (pro bono) or who offers a sliding fee scale.

At the first meeting with your lawyer, make sure that she or he knows what you want and need, and ask whether your goals are realistic. Be honest. Tell your lawyer every fact that is relevant to your situation, especially if you think it may have a negative impact on your case. Bring a short summary of your financial situation and perhaps copies of recent tax returns. You may be asked to give a short history of the marriage, as well as a description of your present situation. Bring a list of questions so you will not forget.

You should ask about the fee at the first meeting, and preferably receive a draft **fee agreement** to take home with you and think about before you sign it. This should spell out the legal work that is undertaken, how the fee is to be computed and how it is to be paid. Most divorce lawyers require a **retainer**, a sum of money on account, before they will agree to take a case. Fees vary widely, depending among other things, upon the lawyer's experience and location. A partner in a Boston law firm may charge over $300 an hour. A sole practitioner in a small town may charge as little as $50 per hour. The average hourly rate is about $150. Be sure to ask for a monthly itemized statement so you can keep track of the costs before the retainer is exhausted.

You may find a lawyer who charges a flat fee for divorce, particularly if it is uncontested. An average flat fee for an uncomplicated, **uncontested divorce** involving custody, support, and property issues is about $1,500. A divorce which requires extensive discovery or negotiation will cost considerably more, even though there is no contested litigation.

A **contested divorce** can be a truly ruinous proposition, financially and otherwise. You will probably not succeed in finding a lawyer to represent you in a contested matter for a flat fee. I have had flat fee agreements with my clients for the past 24 years and I prefer them, but I can understand why most lawyers don't want to risk taking a loss on a case that might drag on and on. However, there ought to be some brakes on run-away divorce lawyers who create piles of unnecessary paperwork, putting the poor parties through all sorts of pointless legal contortions, primarily for the sake of their billable hours.

It is important that your attorney have expertise in family law and in taxes. You may wish to ask how long the lawyer has been in practice, and how much work he or she has done in the area of family law.

Regardless of how you find your lawyer, only you will know if he or she is right for you. Trust your intelligence, your intuition, and your common sense. Don't retain a lawyer you feel uncomfortable with. Many lawyers do not charge for an initial consultation and some will give a reduced rate if asked. You may wish to consult with several attorneys before you make a decision. Be advised that not all lawyers are competent or honest, and some charge undeservedly exorbitant rates. Choose carefully. Here are some typical and telling remarks to help you choose a lawyer or evaluate the one you've got.

Famous Last Words of Lousy Lawyers

"Of course divorce is the only course for you. You've got plenty of grounds, and I suggest we get started right away before he beats you to it."
If the lawyer tries to push you into filing for divorce, or to push you into any other action that you are not ready to take, don't go back.

"Don't worry about a thing. I'll take care of everything."
You may have a hard time getting the lawyer with the large promises to take care of anything, even returning your phone calls.

"Don't even think about my bill. It will come out of the settlement."
You are ultimately responsible for your own lawyer's bill, and it is important that you know from the beginning how it will be computed.

"I'll make all the decisions. Trust me. That's what lawyers are for."
Your lawyer is your advisor and representative, not your boss.

"You're not going to understand any of this, so I won't bother explaining or sending you copies of anything. Why confuse you with the facts?"
You are entitled to know what is happening in your case, and to receive copies of all correspondence and court papers.

"So who needs to negotiate? Let's skip all that and go directly to court! That's the way to get some action!"
Remember, for every action, there is an equal and opposite reaction.

"It's all in who you know, and I know all the judges."
Any lawyer who makes a statement like this is revealing his or her own lack of integrity and competence.

Statements A Competent Lawyer is Likely To Make

"Are you certain that the marriage is over? Have you had counseling? Would you consider a reconciliation?"

"I can't make any promises, but I will make my best effort to secure a reasonable agreement for you. I'll arrange for us to meet with your husband and his lawyer to negotiate a settlement, as soon as financial statements have been exchanged."

"To make sure that we are both clear about the fee agreement, I'll put it in writing, and we'll each have a signed copy."

"I'm accessible. I can almost always return your call by the end of the day. If you have an emergency, be sure to say so when you call."

"I'll send you copies of all the correspondence and pleadings as I receive them, and I will consult with you before taking any action in your case. I also expect you to keep me posted about significant changes."

"A contested divorce is a last resort, and a very difficult process. You're far better off with an agreement, but an agreement does require flexibility and compromise on both sides."

"I'm here to advise you, to inform you, and to represent you, but not to make your decisions for you."

Changing Lawyers

If you become aware that your lawyer is not doing anything on your case or you are dissatisfied for any other reason, you may consider getting a new lawyer. Before you do make a change, it is a good idea to see another lawyer for a second opinion. The delays you are encountering, for example, may not be your lawyer's fault. Some probate courts are tremendously backlogged.

Changing lawyers in the middle of a case should be done only when absolutely necessary. The disadvantages are (1) additional legal fees, (2) additional delay during the transition period, and (3) your new lawyer's lack of first hand knowledge about prior negotiation and/or litigation.

Depending on the fee agreement you originally made with your lawyer, you may be entitled to a refund of part of the retainer. Your former lawyer must return all correspondence and documents to you or your new lawyer upon request, regardless of any outstanding legal fees.

Complaints Against Lawyers

If your lawyer refuses to hand over your file or if you believe that your lawyer has deceived, defrauded, or misled you, you may file a complaint with the Board of Bar Overseers, 11 Beacon Street, Boston, Massachusetts 02108. You may request the complaint by mail or by calling (617) 720-0700. Your lawyer will be required to respond and may be subject to discipline.

However, the Board of Bar Overseers does not deal with issues of malpractice. If your attorney has been incompetent and you have suffered damages as a result, you will need to consult a malpractice attorney, and you should do so even if you think you cannot afford it. A contingency fee agreement is the most common, meaning the malpractice attorney will get up to one third of the damages awarded if you prevail, and nothing if you lose, with expenses paid by you

Fee disputes that do not involve allegations of misconduct may be arbitrated by The Massachusetts Bar Association, Fee Arbitration Board, 20 West Street, Boston, Massachusetts 02111, (617) 542-3602, provided that your lawyer agrees to submit to arbitration.

Chapter 5   OBTAINING A DIVORCE IN MASSACHUSETTS

Residency Requirement

If you and your husband never lived in Massachusetts as a married couple, then you must be a resident for one year before you can file for divorce. You are excepted from this requirement if you are living in Massachusetts at the time that you start the divorce action, and the ground for divorce occurred in Massachusetts.

It is no longer necessary that you and your husband live apart before a divorce action can begin. You may file for divorce before you separate.

Where To File

If you or your husband are still living in the county where you were both last living together, then the divorce action must be filed in the probate court for that county. Otherwise, you may file either in the county where you live or in the county where he lives.

A list of Massachusetts **probate and family courts** is in the Appendix. You may call the divorce department for the forms you need, or go in person. In most counties, a complete package of necessary forms is provided upon request to people who are representing themselves.

Required Documents

In addition to filing a **joint petition** and **affidavit of irretrievable breakdown** (or a **complaint for divorce**), you will be filing the following.

The **marriage certificate**, obtained from the Town Clerk's Office in the town where you were married, or where you got your marriage license.

A **child custody affidavit** is required if there are minor children. This discloses any prior or pending custody actions and the children's whereabouts.

When there are minor children, a graduation **certificate from parenting class** is required in the following counties: Berkshire, Franklin, Hampshire, Hampden, Norfolk, Plymouth and Worcester. The court provides a list of approved programs, and may waive the requirement on motion. The cost is $50.

A **vital statistics form** (form 408) must be filed in all divorces.

The **financial statements** of both parties must be filed before a final hearing will be scheduled. New forms have been promulgated, including an 8 page form for persons earning in excess of $75,000.

The **filing fee** for a divorce is $110.00. An additional $1.00 is required for the summons in all cases except the **joint petition for a no-fault divorce** which does not require a summons. If you cannot afford the filing fee, you can petition the court to waive it. You will be required to complete an **affidavit of indigency,** which like all other forms is obtained from the divorce department of the probate court.

Chapter 6   THE UNCONTESTED DIVORCE

An **uncontested divorce** is one that is settled between the parties prior to a final hearing, generally with a written separation agreement.

Choose Grounds

It is important to note that both **uncontested** and **contested** divorces can be heard on either **fault** grounds or **no-fault** grounds. There are 7 fault grounds, described in detail in Chapter 8, but most fault divorce complaints are filed on the ground of **cruel and abusive treatment,** which means that the abusive conduct of one spouse has had a detrimental effect on the physical or mental well-being of the other spouse.

The no-fault ground is **irretrievable breakdown of the marriage** meaning reconciliation is impossible. There are two types of no-fault divorce, governed by Massachusetts General Laws chapter 208, Sections 1A and 1B. You must decide before filing whether your divorce will be an uncontested "1A" no-fault divorce, or a contested no-fault divorce, also called a "1B" divorce. The law requires you to wait six months after filing the complaint before a hearing can be scheduled on the "1B" divorce. You may change your grounds for divorce by filing a motion to amend the complaint prior to the hearing, or at the hearing if your spouse assents.

If you and your husband have already signed a **separation agreement,** you will most likely file a **joint petition for a "1A" no-fault divorce.** If, however, you have not yet signed a separation agreement with your husband, you may prefer to file a fault divorce complaint so that you retain the option of introducing evidence concerning marital conduct, in the event that a separation agreement cannot be reached. There are several other factors which may influence your choice of grounds.

Both parties are required to be present at the final hearing on a **joint petition for a no-fault divorce** and it is necessary to have a separation agreement. In an uncontested fault divorce, only the **plaintiff** (the person filing the divorce complaint) needs to be present at the final hearing, and it is not necessary to have a separation agreement, although it is preferable.

There is a longer waiting period for the divorce judgment to become final on a "1A" no-fault divorce, namely 120 days, as opposed to 90 days for a divorce judgment to become final in a fault divorce or a "1B" no fault divorce.

You may wish to wait until you know whether or not you and your husband can reach an agreement before you decide which grounds to use, and file for divorce. Regardless of the grounds for divorce, it is necessary to exchange financial statements with your husband, and to reach a separation agreement before you can have an uncontested final hearing.

Exchange of Financial Statements and Mandatory Self-Disclosure

The law requires that there be complete and mutual financial disclosure between husband and wife before the making of an agreement. Each party is required to file a financial statement with the court, and to exchange copies

16

with the other within 45 days of service of the summons, or at least two business days before any hearing. Financial statements may also be requested upon 10 days notice in a formal pleading called a Request for a Financial Statement, with mandatory sanctions for non-compliance, except for good cause.

See the Appendix for copies of the newly revised financial statements which now come in two forms. The traditional pink 2 page financial statement is now reserved for those with incomes of less than $75,000. Those earning $75,000 or more must complete a lilac 8 page form.

It is now necessary that the attorney of record co-sign the financial statement affirming that she or he has no knowledge of any false information, and disclosing the legal fees being incurred.

There is also a new Supplementary Rule 410 on **Mandatory Self-Disclosure.** Unless the parties agree otherwise, each must deliver to the other, with 45 days of service of the summons, the past 3 years' federal and state tax returns, W-2s, 1099s, bank statements and statements for all securities, CDs, 401(K), IRA and pension plans, as well as any loan or mortgage applications and financial statements. The four most recent pay stubs from each employer must also be provided, along with health insurance information, and there is a continuing duty to supplement the information.

Reach a Separation Agreement

After financial statements have been exchanged, negotiation begins. Often written proposals for a settlement are made. Generally there are also meetings, either just between the two attorneys or among all four parties.
Separation agreements and ways of reaching them are discussed in Chapter 7, which also includes a sample separation agreement on pages 24-29. Once a separation agreement has been reached, it is customary to file a **joint petition for a "1A" no-fault divorce.**

UNCONTESTED NO-FAULT DIVORCE PROCEDURE

File the Joint Petition and related documents.

An uncontested no-fault divorce involves the filing of a **joint petition for divorce,** a copy of the **marriage certificate,** a **vital statistics form,** the **financial statements** of both parties, a notarized **affidavit of irretrievable breakdown of the marriage,** and a $110 filing fee made out to "Register of Probate". If there are minor children (under age 18), a child custody affidavit must also be filed. The **separation agreement** is generally filed at the same time as the "1A" petition and other documents listed above, although it may be filed later. See the Appendix for sample forms.

Parenting Class

In Berkshire, Franklin, Hampshire, Hampden, Norfolk, Plymouth and Worcester, it is now necessary to attend **parenting class,** if there are minor children. The cost is $50 for two 2½ hour sessions which you and your husband attend separately. You then receive a **certificate of attendance** which must be filed with the court before a hearing can be scheduled.

17

Request a Hearing

A hearing can be requested as soon as all of the above documents have been filed with the probate court. See the Appendix for a sample **trial request** form, which you send to the Trial Department at the Probate Court. You will generally receive a hearing notice from the court within a month.

The Hearing

You will receive your notice of the hearing approximately 2 weeks in advance of the hearing date. The notice will state the time that you must be in court. When you arrive, ask the court officer where the list of cases is posted. You will find your name on the list, and it will indicate the right courtroom. Check in with the clerk and file any additional papers, such as an **updated financial statement**. If there is no change in your finances, you must sign an additional copy of your last financial statement and date it the day of the hearing. When the clerk reads your name at the **call of the list**, stand up and answer, "here." You must then wait your turn to be heard. When your name is called again, walk up to the bench where you will be sworn in by the clerk.

If you are represented by a lawyer, he or she will ask you to state to the judge all the information included in your **joint petition for divorce**. You will be asked whether you believe that there is an **irretrievable breakdown** of your marriage. Then, you will be asked whether you wish the court to approve the separation agreement that you and your husband have executed.

If you are representing yourself, you will be giving the above information directly to the judge. The following is a suggested statement for a no-fault divorce.

"My name is Molly Brown."
"My address is 39 Lilac Court, Cambridge."
"I am married to Desmond Brown of 19 Leonard Avenue, Cambridge."
"We were married on June 19, 1982 at Concord, Massachusetts."
"We last lived together in Cambridge on January 3, 1998."
"We have two children, Stephen born August 12, 1983 and Michael born
    August 18, 1989."
"The children live with me, and they see their father often."
"I feel that our marriage has broken down irretrievably."
"We tried marriage counseling, but we both came to realize that there
    is no possibility of reconciliation."
"We signed an agreement in October, after each of us consulted with lawyers."
"I have read and I understand all provisions of the agreement and I feel that
    it is fair and reasonable."
"The agreement provides that we have joint legal custody of the boys and I
    have physical custody."
"Mr. Brown pays child support pursuant to the guidelines and provides medical
    insurance for us all."
"All property has been divided and Mr. Brown will be paying the cost of the
    children's education."

The judge may ask you specific questions about the separation agreement, such as how much support you will be receiving, how the property is distributed, and whether the custody arrangements are satisfactory. The judge may also ask whether the agreement survives as a contract or not, and whether you understand what this means. See Chapter 7.

Your husband will then be asked whether he also believes the marriage has broken down irretrievably, and whether he too wishes the court to approve the separation agreement. The amount of time an uncontested no-fault divorce requires is approximately 5 to 10 minutes.

The Divorce Judgment

You will receive a copy of the judge's order approving the separation agreement in about a week. A **judgment nisi** (conditional divorce judgment) is issued 30 days after the hearing and becomes final in an additional 90 days. You will not receive notice of the entry of the **final judgment of divorce**. However, you may obtain a certified copy by writing to the Register of Probate 120 days after the hearing, giving the **docket number** of your case and enclosing $10.00.

UNCONTESTED FAULT DIVORCE PROCEDURE

File The Complaint

This action is commenced by filing a fault **divorce complaint** along with the $111.00 **filing fee**, the **marriage certificate**, the **child custody affidavit**, and the **vital statistics form**. A sample fault divorce complaint alleging cruel and abusive treatment is in the Appendix.

Cruel and abusive treatment is the most commonly used fault ground. It involves abusive conduct on one spouse's part that has a detrimental effect on the other. The abuse need not be physical, and no proof is required. In an uncontested fault divorce, your uncorroborated testimony is sufficient to establish grounds. Other fault grounds are described in Chapter 8.

Serve Copies of the Complaint and Summons

About a week after the divorce complaint has been filed, you will receive a **summons** from the court. This is the official notice to your husband that you have started a divorce action. Your husband must be served with copies of the complaint and summons. This is called **service of process.**

Copies of the divorce complaint and summons may be served on your husband by a **sheriff** or **constable.** The service can also be made by a **disinterested person** who is not a party to the lawsuit. The constable will personally deliver to your husband his copy of the divorce complaint and summons, and then sign the original summons **proof of service.**

Alternatively, your husband may voluntarily **accept service** by signing the original summons before a notary public, who also signs.

If you cannot locate your husband, you may serve him by publication in the newspaper selected by the court for the area where he last resided. Request a **summons by publication** when you file your complaint.

Return the Original Summons to the Court

The original summons indicating when, where, and how your husband has been served, and signed by the person who served him, must be returned to the court. This is called **return of service**.

Request a Hearing

You must wait 20 days after the summons has been served before you can request a hearing. This allows the **defendant** time to file an **answer** NS **counterclaim** to the complaint, if he wishes to do so. This indicates that he may contest the divorce. If a separation agreement has been reached, it is not likely that the defendant will be filing an answer, but 20 days must elapse anyway before you can request a hearing. A sample **trial request** form is in the Appendix. In some counties, as described above, you may also need a certificate of **attendance at parenting class**.

The Hearing

You will be notified by mail of the date and time of the hearing. The uncontested fault hearing is identical to the no-fault hearing described above, except that you will be testifying about your ground for divorce, instead of testifying about the irretrievable breakdown of your marriage. You will be asked to give a brief statement of the facts which constitute your ground for divorce. Describe the actual events which led to your separation from your husband. The judge will let you know when he or she has heard sufficient testimony. It will not be necessary to go into great detail.

The Divorce Judgment

A **judgment of divorce nisi** (conditional) will be entered on the day of your hearing, and you will receive a copy in about a week. The judgment of divorce will become final 90 days after the hearing with no additional notice to you. You may order a certified copy of your **final divorce judgment** from the Register of Probate at the court for $10.00.

You may not remarry during the 90 day wait, or **nisi** period. However, all the provisions relating to support, custody, etc. are effective on the day of your hearing. If you and your husband signed a separation agreement before the hearing, the provisions went into effect on the date that the last person signed, known as the date that the agreement was made or executed.

Chapter 7   THE SEPARATION AGREEMENT

A **separation agreement** is a written contract between you and your husband. Its purpose is to settle all the issues of your divorce, such as custody of minor children, visits, support, property settlement, and insurance. As with any contract, a separation agreement requires negotiation and compromise. The process generally takes several weeks, but can take months or even years. Eventually, 90% of all divorces in Massachusetts are concluded by agreement.

If you are representing yourself, it is important that you consult a lawyer **before** you arrive at an agreement, preferably before you start negotiating. At the very least, for your own protection, consult a lawyer before you sign an agreement with your husband. Once you sign your name, it may be impossible to change the terms you agreed to.

If you are being represented by a lawyer, make sure she or he knows exactly what you need. It is best to give your lawyer a list of those items that are most important to you, as well as items which are negotiable.

Complete financial disclosure is necessary for a valid separation agreement. You and your husband should exchange financial statements a reasonable time before the agreement is concluded to allow time for review. If possible, statements should be exchanged at the beginning of negotiation, even though both parties may already be familiar with each other's finances.

Ways of Reaching a Separation Agreement

Negotiating Through Attorneys

There are many different ways to reach a separation agreement, and most attorneys use a combination of meetings, telephone calls, and correspondence. One of the most effective ways is for wife, husband, and the two lawyers to meet to discuss and resolve issues in a **4-way meeting.**

With all parties present, there is no lack of information or feedback to slow down the negotiation process. It is always possible to go off and caucus with your lawyer privately for a few minutes if you need, for example, to discuss a new suggestion for settlement.

Some people, including some attorneys, refuse to participate in a 4-way meeting, because of the high degree of emotional tension that is often present. But, the trauma of a meeting is minimal compared to that of a contested divorce. Also, the court mandates a 4-way meeting prior to the pre-trial conference, or pursuant to a case management conference.

Written proposals for settlement can also be made back and forth between the parties. This is a good way to negotiate when distance is a factor. It has the advantage over telephone calls in eliminating confusion about what was proposed and/or accepted to date.

Negotiating On Your Own

If you are representing yourself, you can use a combination of meetings, written offers of settlement, or phone calls to try to reach agreement with your husband. Again, it is important that you consult with a family lawyer **before** you start to represent yourself. You will have to compromise in order to reach an agreement, and a lawyer can advise you on the reasonableness of the concessions you may be considering. Be sure to have a lawyer review, and preferably draft, your separation agreement before you sign it.

Even if you have a lawyer, it is best to keep an open line of communication with your husband. Nothing prevents the two of you from reaching an agreement at any time during the negotiation.

Mediation

Another method of reaching a separation agreement is **divorce mediation.** A **mediator**, generally but not necessarily an attorney, meets with husband and wife on several occasions in an attempt to settle the issues in dispute, such as custody, child support or property division. The mediator represents neither spouse, but strives to be a neutral, objective third party. The mediator's fee, generally an hourly rate from $50 to $250, is shared equally by husband and wife, or is shared in proportion to their respective incomes.

It is most important to **consult an attorney before you start a mediation process,** so that you have a clear idea of what your legal rights and responsibilities are ahead of time. That way you will be able to formulate realistic goals. **Consult a lawyer again before you sign a mediated agreement.**

If and when an agreement is reached through mediation, a memorandum of the agreement is prepared by the mediator. Each spouse then takes the memorandum to his or her own attorney for review. One of the attorneys drafts the separation agreement. The other attorney reviews it. Sometimes the mediator drafts the agreement. An uncontested divorce follows.

Successful mediation can result in savings in legal fees to both parties. Mediation, however, is not necessarily a satisfactory option. This is especially true when one spouse is uninformed or is intimidated by the other. Sometimes the mediator is also uninformed or is incompetent, or easily persuaded by the more forceful spouse. The result can be a very one-sided agreement.

Unsuccessful mediation can significantly increase both the cost of your divorce, and the length of time required to conclude it. To increase your chances of success, you may choose a mediator who is an attorney with extensive experience in divorce, and with a working knowledge of taxes.

Unfortunately, because there are no regulations or licensing requirements yet, there are many self-proclaimed "divorce mediators" with little or no knowledge of divorce law or taxes. In their ignorance, they do much damage, for example, by advising divorcing couples to sign agreements that have not been reviewed by attorneys for both parties.

Most counties provide free or low cost mediation services through the probate and family court. The quality of mediation provided is often as good as or better than that of expensive private mediators.

A good mediator will encourage you and your husband to each consult with your own lawyers, before, during, and after the mediation process.

After Some Litigation

Many divorce cases which start with contested litigation, because of emergencies requiring temporary orders, are concluded by agreement. You may, for example, have obtained temporary orders for support and custody, and then after a cooling off period, decided to work out the details of a settlement with your husband, on your own or through attorneys.

An agreement can be reached at any stage of litigation, even once the final contested hearing on the merits has begun. Approximately 80% of all cases which reach the **pre-trial hearing** stage are settled in court at that time. See Chapter 8.

The Provisions of a Separation Agreement

Once you and your husband have agreed in principle on all the issues, your lawyer (or his) will put together a first draft of a separation agreement. Sometimes there are several drafts before the final, mutually acceptable, draft is signed.

The sample separation agreement which follows involves a hypothetical family with two minor children, ages 10 and 4. The wife and the husband both work, and own the family home, which is the only asset of the marriage.

Molly and Desmond want the children to be able to stay in the family home until they graduate from high school. When both children have graduated, the home will be sold.

Desmond is required by law to share his pension, accumulated during the marriage, with Molly. He is also required to continue existing medical insurance for Molly and the children.

Desmond and Molly are following the **Child Support Guidelines** to determine support, but agree to a 30% reduction in child support when Stephen, their oldest, goes to college. This is because Desmond has agreed to pay all college expenses.

Although they have tried to provide for every contingency, Molly and Desmond will be able to return to court to seek a modification of any provision having to do with the children. However, Article 6 provides that, except as to matters concerning the children, the agreement survives as an independent contract.

This means that, unless fraud or duress in the making of the agreement can be proved, it will be virtually impossible to change the property division or alimony provisions.

23

SEPARATION AGREEMENT

This Agreement between MOLLY BROWN of Cambridge, Middlesex County, Massachusetts, hereinafter called the WIFE, and DESMOND BROWN of Cambridge, Middlesex County, Massachusetts, hereinafter called the HUSBAND, is made this 21st day of October, 1998. **The date is that of the last to sign.**

STATEMENT OF FACTS

A. The HUSBAND and the WIFE were lawfully married on June 19, 1982 at Concord, Massachusetts. There are two children of the marriage, namely STEPHEN, born August 12, 1983, and MICHAEL, born August 18, 1989.

B. Serious and irreconcilable differences have arisen between the HUSBAND and the WIFE, and the parties are living apart from one another.

C. The purpose of this Agreement is to remove the subject matter hereof from litigation, and to make a final and complete determination as to the care and maintenance of the children, the respective property rights of the HUSBAND and the WIFE, and all other matters which should be settled in view of the separation of the parties.

D. The HUSBAND and the WIFE have each had independent legal advice by counsel of his or her own selection. Each fully understands the facts and has been fully informed of all legal rights and liabilities. After such advice and knowledge, each believes the Agreement to be fair, just, and reasonable; and each signs the Agreement freely and voluntarily.

NOW, THEREFORE, in consideration of the mutual promises, agreements and covenants hereinafter contained, the HUSBAND and the WIFE mutually agree as follows. **This recital of consideration is an essential element of any contract, recording an exchange for value between the parties.**

1. AUTONOMY OF THE PARTIES

From the date of this Agreement, the HUSBAND and the WIFE may continue to live separate and apart from one another for the rest of their lives, as if sole and unmarried. **Molly and Desmond are now free to live their own lives, as if they were single, except they cannot remarry until the divorce is final.**

2. WAIVER OF CLAIMS

The HUSBAND and the WIFE hereby mutually release and forever discharge each other from any and all actions, suits, debts, claims, demands, and obligations whatsoever, both in law and in equity, which either of them has ever had, now has, or may hereafter have against the other, by reason of any matter up to the date of the Agreement, it being the intention of the parties that henceforth there shall exist as between them only such rights and obligations as are specifically provided for in this Agreement. **This document covers everything Molly and Desmond agreed to, and they waive all other claims.**

3. WAIVER OF INHERITANCE AND PROPERTY RIGHTS

The HUSBAND and the WIFE each hereby waive all rights of inheritance at law or in equity. Each hereby waives, renounces and relinquishes all and every interest which either may now have in any real or personal property of the other. **Inheritance rights (described in Chapter 12) are lost when the**

24

divorce becomes final in any event. This Agreement establishes the couple's property rights, and the distribution is final.

4. WAIVER OF RIGHTS PURSUANT TO M.G.L. C.208, SEC. 34
Both parties waive all rights pursuant to Massachusetts General Laws chapter 208, section 34 to seek an additional distribution of property, and are satisfied that the division of property made herein is fair, just, and equitable.

Both parties specifically waive all rights to alimony, past, present and future. **Molly and Desmond are waiving all rights to return to court for additional property or for alimony. A copy of the statute is in the Appendix.**

5. INTEGRATION OF AGREEMENT
The HUSBAND and the WIFE have incorporated in this Agreement their entire understanding. The parties agree that there have not been made, and that they have not relied upon, any promises, warranties, or representations, except as expressly contained herein. **There are no outside agreements.**

6. INCORPORATION OF AGREEMENT IN DIVORCE JUDGMENT
At a hearing on the divorce complaint of either party, a copy of this Agreement shall be submitted to the Court and incorporated in the judgment by leave of the Court. The parties intend that, except as to provisions relating to the children, this Agreement shall not be merged in the decree, but shall survive the same as an independent contract and be forever binding upon the HUSBAND and the WIFE and their heirs, executors, administrators and assigns for all time.

All separation agreements are incorporated in the divorce judgment after the hearing, meaning that the judgment refers to and includes the terms of the separation agreement. Some separation agreements provide that the agreement shall also survive as an independent contract between the parties. This means it is the intention of the parties that no changes be made in the agreement by a court in the future. Other separation agreements do not survive the divorce judgment, but are merged in it, meaning that a court may, at a later date, make changes in an action for modification.

If the separation agreement is silent on whether it is to survive or not, then it is deemed to survive as a binding, independent contract.

7. MODIFICATION OF AGREEMENT
This Agreement shall not be altered or modified except by an instrument signed and acknowledged by the HUSBAND and the WIFE. **Any changes Desmond and Molly agree to must be in writing.**

8. UNIMPAIRED FORCE OF AGREEMENT IN EVENT OF DEFAULT
The failure of the HUSBAND or of the WIFE to insist in any instance upon the strict performance of any of the terms hereof, or to provide notice to the other of the other's default hereunder shall not be construed as a waiver of such term or terms and the same shall nevertheless continue in full force and effect. **All provisions of the Agreement remain in effect even though one party may neglect to fulfill his obligations for a period of time.**

9. INVALIDITY OF A PROVISION
In the event any part of this Agreement shall be held invalid, such invalidity shall not affect the whole Agreement, but the remaining provisions

of this Agreement shall continue to be valid and binding to the extent that such provisions continue to reflect fairly the intent and understanding of the parties. **In case the law changes and as a result one provision in your Agreement becomes invalid, the other provisions will remain valid.**

10. APPLICABLE LAW

This Agreement shall be construed and governed according to the laws of the Commonwealth of Massachusetts. **Family law differs from state to state, but the Agreement will be governed by Massachusetts law regardless of where the parties may live.**

11. CUSTODY OF THE CHILDREN

The parties agree that they will share legal custody of the minor children, and will consult each other prior to making any major decision concerning each child's medical care, religious upbringing, education, extracurricular activities, and travel. The children will make their home with the WIFE and the WIFE shall have physical custody of the children. **Most divorcing parents share joint legal custody of children under 18, except in extreme circumstances. However, it is customary for one parent to have physical custody. This will usually be the parent who has had the primary responsibility for the care of the children, and most often this is still the mother. Both parties shall have the right to medical and school records of the children, and the parties shall keep each other informed of the health and academic progress of the children.**

The HUSBAND and the WIFE shall each at all times encourage and foster in the children respect and affection for the other and shall cooperate with each other in all matters concerning their children, so that the children will have the continued benefit of the care and affection of both parents. **Desmond and Molly agree to keep each other informed and to work together for the sake of their children.**

12. VISITS WITH THE CHILDREN

The HUSBAND shall have the right and opportunity to visit with the children at all reasonable times. The HUSBAND shall provide the WIFE with reasonable notice of visits. **Molly and Desmond will be flexible and considerate about visits. See the Appendix for the Massachusetts Bar Foundation's excellent guidelines for visits.**

13. SUPPORT OF THE CHILDREN

The HUSBAND shall, this day and each week hereafter, pay to the WIFE for the support of the children the sum of Two Hundred Seventeen Dollars ($217), pursuant to the child support guidelines. The parties agree to exchange W-2 and 1099 forms on March 1 of each year hereafter to recompute the amount of child support, unless they both agree otherwise. **Some people prefer to recompute child support each year or every time there is a raise or job change. Others prefer to keep the status quo and not exchange financial information on a regular basis.**

The HUSBAND'S child support obligation shall be reduced by thirty per cent (30%) when STEPHEN reaches the age of eighteen (18) or graduates from high school, whichever occurs last, and shall cease when MICHAEL reaches the age of eighteen (18) or graduates from high school. **This reduction takes into account both Molly's reduced expenses when Michael alone is home, and the fact that Desmond will be paying for Stephen's college expenses.**

26

Alternatively they might have agreed that Desmond would keep paying child support pursuant to the guidelines, but that he and Molly would share the children's college expenses in proportion to their gross incomes.

14. CHILDREN AS DEPENDENTS FOR INCOME TAX PURPOSES

The WIFE shall not claim nor consider the children as dependents for the purpose of filing her annual federal or state income taxes for any calendar year, and shall execute all documents which the HUSBAND deems necessary to enable him to so claim the children, including IRS Form 8332. **Molly is agreeing to give up her right (as a custodial parent) to claim the children as dependents. Since Desmond earns $45,000 and Molly earns $29,000, these exemptions result in a greater tax savings for him than they would for her. Also, the real estate deductions (for interest and taxes paid) give Molly substantial income tax benefits.**

15. MEDICAL INSURANCE AND UNINSURED EXPENSES

The HUSBAND shall maintain the present medical insurance coverage for the benefit of the WIFE and the minor children, so long as they remain eligible. In the event that there is an additional cost for the WIFE'S coverage, the WIFE shall be responsible for payment of it. The HUSBAND'S obligation to provide medical insurance coverage for the WIFE shall continue so long as she remains eligible under the terms of the present plan.

The HUSBAND shall pay the cost of uninsured medical expenses of the children. The WIFE shall pay the cost of uninsured dental expenses of the children. **Desmond is required by law to maintain existing medical insurance for Molly and the children so long as they remain eligible. Generally the end of full-time student status terminates eligibility for children and remarriage terminates the eligibility of a former spouse.**

16. EDUCATION OF THE CHILDREN

The HUSBAND agrees that he will contribute to the college education of each child an amount equivalent to the annual cost of tuition, room and board at the University of Massachusetts at Amherst. The obligation of the HUSBAND shall be limited to four (4) academic years per child, and shall terminate when each child reaches age twenty-three (23). The parties agree that they will co-operate with each other in all applications and procedures which are required to obtain additional financial assistance for the children's education. **This provision guarantees that Stephen and Michael will be able to count on a college education. It eliminates any need for negotiations about college costs and sets a realistic amount that Desmond has obligated himself to provide. If the children wish to attend private colleges, they and Molly will have to come up with the additional funds required.**

17. LIFE INSURANCE

The HUSBAND agrees to maintain the presently existing life insurance policy, number 019957-2685, in the amount of Two Hundred Thousand Dollars ($200,000) with the Fireman's Field Day Insurance Company, and to name the children as sole and irrevocable beneficiaries of the policy. The HUSBAND further agrees that upon request of the WIFE, he will provide her with annual proof of the continued existence of the policy. The obligation of the HUSBAND hereunder shall cease when the youngest child reaches age twenty-three (23), or graduates from college whichever occurs first. **This provision insures that there will be enough money for the support and education of the children.**

27

18. INDIVIDUAL DEBTS
Neither the HUSBAND nor the WIFE shall hereafter contract or incur any debt, charge or liability for which the other or the other's property or estate may become liable. At the time of this Agreement, there are no outstanding bills incurred by either party which are the obligation of the other, except as provided by this Agreement. Each of the parties further covenants at all times to hold the other free, harmless and indemnified from and against all debts, charges or liabilities previously contracted or incurred or hereafter contracted or incurred in breach of the provisions of this Article, and from any and all attorney's fees, costs and expenses incurred by the non-breaching party as a result of any such breach. **Molly and Desmond have divided up all their bills and credit cards, and each will be responsible for their own future expenses.**

19. DIVISION OF PERSONAL PROPERTY
The HUSBAND and the WIFE covenant that all personal property owned jointly and severally by them has already been divided between them. **Desmond and Molly have divided all their possessions, including all joint accounts.**

20. REAL ESTATE
The HUSBAND and the WIFE own jointly the real estate known and numbered as 39 Lilac Court, Cambridge, Middlesex County, Massachusetts, title to which is recorded at Middlesex South Registry of Deeds at Book 45789, Page 000.

The parties agree that the WIFE shall have sole use and occupancy of said real estate, and shall be responsible for expenses of same, including but not limited to mortgage principal and interest, real estate tax, utilities, and routine maintenance. The parties shall consult together and shall share equally the cost of any reasonable and necessary repairs over Two Hundred Dollars ($200).

On or before June 1, 2007, the parties shall place said real estate on the market, and shall cooperate with each other in all matters required to effect a sale. The WIFE shall receive sixty percent (60%) of the net proceeds of sale, and the HUSBAND shall receive forty percent (40%). **Molly and Desmond are agreeing that she can live in the house with the children until Michael, the youngest, is age 18, then they will sell it and split the proceeds 60% to Molly and 40% to Desmond. This split is made in consideration of Desmond's greater earning power and the waiver of alimony.**

21. PENSION
The HUSBAND and the WIFE agree to share equally all funds accumulated to date in the HUSBAND'S pension with Fly By Night Airlines, the HUSBAND'S employer. The parties agree further that upon the retirement of the HUSBAND, the WIFE shall receive, directly from HUSBAND'S said employer, a proportionate distribution of all benefits payable to HUSBAND, pursuant to a Qualified Domestic Relations Order.

The WIFE'S percentage of said benefits shall be equal to one half ($\frac{1}{2}$) the present value of said pension, plus accumulated interest thereon until the retirement of the HUSBAND, divided by the total value of said pension and all interest thereon at the time of the HUSBAND'S retirement. **Equal division of all pensions accumulated during the marriage is required by law. However, there can be a trade-off against other assets of the marriage. If the pension itself is to be divided, the judge should be asked to sign the Q.D.R.O. at the final hearing.**

22. <u>TAX RETURNS</u>

The HUSBAND and the WIFE agree to file joint state and federal income tax returns for the calendar year 1998 and to share any refund in proportion to their gross incomes. The HUSBAND and the WIFE warrant to each other that they have each fairly reported their incomes and allowable credits and deductions on all joint returns filed by them, that their tax payments are current, and that there are no pending notices of audit or tax deficiency proceedings. Each party agrees that upon receipt of any such notice he or she will immediately notify the other in writing. Each party shall be responsible for any deficiency related to his or her own income. Any other deficiencies shall be shared by the parties in proportion to their gross incomes. **Generally divorcing couples save money by filing jointly. If however you suspect your husband is filing a false return, you should file as a "married person filing separately" or, if you have children, "head of household."**

This Agreement is executed in five duplicate originals, one each to be retained by the Court, the HUSBAND, the WIFE, and their respective attorneys. **Molly and Desmond will each sign the original and 4 copies of their Agreement before a notary.**

IN WITNESS WHEREOF, the parties hereunto set their hands and seals and have each initialed each of the foregoing pages.

_____   _____
Molly Brown   Desmond Brown

COMMONWEALTH OF MASSACHUSETTS

Middlesex County   October 19, 1998

Then personally appeared the above-named MOLLY BROWN, to me known to be the person described herein, who executed the foregoing instrument, and who acknowledged that she executed the same as her own free act and deed before me

_____
Notary Public
My Commission Expires: 11-23-2003

COMMONWEALTH OF MASSACHUSETTS

Middlesex County   October 21, 1998

Then personally appeared the above-named DESMOND BROWN, to me known to be the person described herein, who executed the foregoing instrument, and who acknowledged that he executed the same as his own free act and deed, before me

_____
Notary Public
My Commission Expires: 11-23-2003

Chapter 8   THE CONTESTED DIVORCE

If it is impossible for you to reach an agreement with your husband, then you may be one of the relatively small percentage of people who have a contested divorce. This can be a very difficult experience, especially when there are children. Contested divorce is expensive, time consuming, and traumatic. It does not necessarily lead to a satisfactory result.

However, if your husband tries to avoid his responsibilities toward you or toward the children or refuses to negotiate a reasonable separation agreement, you will need to litigate issues. If at all possible, you should be represented by competent legal counsel. It is very difficult to represent yourself in a contested divorce.

Procedure

The initial procedure for a contested divorce is identical to that of the uncontested fault divorce described in Chapter 6. You **file the complaint, serve the complaint and summons,** and **make return of service.** Then, if an agreement cannot be reached, you **request a pre-trial hearing.**

Grounds: Fault or No-Fault?

As with uncontested divorce, it is first necessary to decide whether your grounds for divorce will be fault or no-fault.

Chapter 208, section 1B provides that a **divorce complaint** can be filed on the ground of **irretrievable breakdown of the marriage** without the consent of the other spouse. However, it is necessary to wait six months after the filing of the **"1B" no-fault divorce complaint** before a final hearing. Unlike the contested fault divorce, the issue of marital conduct is generally excluded in the trial of a "1B" contested no-fault divorce. A contested divorce is often filed on one of the 7 following **fault grounds.**

Cruel and Abusive Treatment This is the most common fault ground for divorce. It involves conduct on one spouse's part that has a detrimental physical effect on the other spouse, such as weight loss or gain, inability to sleep or work, nervousness, depression or injury. It is not necessary that actual physical abuse occur. The abusive conduct may also be verbal harassment, mental cruelty, adultery or refusal to communicate.

Adultery The ground of adultery refers to sexual intercourse with a person of the opposite sex outside of marriage. Use of this ground by parents is not favored by the courts because of the adverse impact of the record on the children. The clerk or the judge may ask you to change the ground of adultery to cruel and abusive treatment if you have children. Adultery is usually proved by circumstantial evidence. "Adulterous disposition" and "opportunity to commit adultery" are the elements which must be proven. Although your husband may have admitted that he slept with another woman, if possible you should provide the time, place, and/or circumstances of your husband's adultery. If your husband was found to be the father of another woman's child in a paternity suit, this is sufficient proof. If he is actually living with another woman, he is presumed to be guilty of adultery.

Impotency This means the inability to have sexual intercourse, **not** the inability to have a child, which is infertility. You have to prove that your husband is unable (not just unwilling) to have intercourse, that the condition existed at the time of the marriage and was unknown to you, and that it is probably incurable.

Desertion You must show that your husband abandoned you without justification or provocation, and that you haven't lived together for one year prior to filing for divorce. The desertion must be against your consent. There is no desertion if you both agree to live apart or you are living apart under a separate support order. It does not make a difference if your husband is voluntarily sending you money, so long as he left you against your will.

Gross and Confirmed Habits of Intoxication You must prove that the habit of intoxication, by excessive use of drugs or alcohol, existed at the time you filed the divorce complaint.

Non-Support The ground of non-support is a narrow one. You must prove that your husband has the means to support you, that he refuses to do so, and that his refusal to provide you with the necessities of life is gross, wanton and cruel. If you have received an eviction notice for non-payment of rent or utility shut off notices, you should bring these to court with you as evidence of non-support.

Sentence to Prison or Jail for More Than Five Years There is no requirement as to the amount of time that must actually be served in prison, as long as the sentence was for 5 years or more. This ground may be used even if the sentence was suspended. You will need to get a certified copy of your husband's conviction from the court in which he was tried and bring this copy with you to the divorce hearing.

Defenses to Complaint for Divorce

Your husband can try to prevent you from getting a divorce on fault grounds by successfully defending himself against the ground which you have accused him of in your complaint. He may do this by filing an **answer** to your complaint for divorce, raising one or more of the following defenses.

He may **deny** that you have grounds for divorce. He may state that he was **insane** at the time he committed the alleged acts. He may claim that you were in **collusion** with him, that you both agreed to make up a ground for divorce where none existed. He may claim **condonation**, meaning you forgave the acts which constitute your grounds for divorce, by word or deed, such as living or sleeping with him after the act occurred. He may claim that you are guilty of **connivance**, meaning you urged him to commit the act you are complaining of, for example, adultery. If your husband succeeds in proving any of the above defenses, the divorce may not be granted. However, it is rare for a judge not to grant a divorce regardless of the defense raised.

Your husband's **answer** may contain a **counterclaim**, his opposing claim for divorce against you. Alternatively, he may file his own complaint for divorce called a **cross-complaint**. The procedure is the same as for the original divorce complaint, except that another marriage certificate is not required. The two complaints share the same docket number and are heard together. The judge may grant each party a divorce at the final hearing.

Rather than contest the divorce itself, your husband may contest your request for custody, support or a property settlement. A contest over the issues is much more common than a contest over grounds. An **answer** is almost always filed when the defendant contests any aspect of the divorce, including grounds, custody and financial issues. The defendant's lawyer will file an **appearance** with the court, which establishes as a matter of record that he or she represents your husband.

It is possible for a defendant or his attorney to **appear specially** for the limited purpose of contesting the court's right to hear the case because of improper service of the summons, insufficient residence of the plaintiff in Massachusetts, or the fact that another court has already assumed jurisdiction in the matter, for example. The court will then decide whether it has jurisdiction to hear the case.

Temporary Orders

A contested divorce often begins with litigation over temporary orders. Temporary orders may be granted after the complaint for divorce has been filed. A temporary restraining order, a temporary custody order, an order to vacate the marital home, and an attachment of real or personal property may be made before service of a summons only if advance notice to your husband would result in irreparable harm.

Personal service on your husband is required before the court can issue an order for temporary support. A deputy sheriff, constable or disinterested person should serve him with the divorce complaint and summons and your motion for temporary support. If he has already been personally served with the divorce papers, you may simply send him the motion for temporary support as described below.

You may mark a case for hearing on temporary orders by calling or writing to the **motions clerk** of the Probate Court asking that the case be marked on a date that you select. You may have to wait several weeks, due to backlog.

The rules have been recently amended to require that every motion be accompanied by a **proposed order,** which is served with the motion. The proposed order sets forth in numbered paragraphs the relief sought.

It is necessary on all motions for temporary orders to send a copy of your motion and proposed order to your husband or his lawyer at least 10 days before the hearing date you have selected, or you may arrange to serve the motion in hand at least 7 days before the hearing. It is generally a good idea to use both first class mail and certified mail, return receipt requested, so that you will have the necessary proof in case of dispute.

There is an emergency exception to the 10 days (by mail) or 7 days personal service requirement. You must attach an **affidavit** signed under penalties of perjury listing the specific reasons why you believe that immediate and irreparable harm will result if you are not granted a temporary restraining, custody or vacate order without notice. The judge will generally issue an emergency temporary order which is good for 5 to 10 days, and which is reviewed before the end of this time in a hearing with your husband present. You must give your husband regular notice of this hearing, and also mail him a copy of the order of the court.

Opposing motions, along with accompanying proposed orders and affidavits must be served at least 2 business days before the hearing.

Temporary Restraining Order

A **temporary restraining order** prohibits your husband from abusing you or imposing any restraint on your personal liberty, or from taking other action, such as selling property.

Generally, when the relief sought is protection from physical abuse or threats of abuse, it is preferable to use the "209A" procedure described on pages 4 and 5. There is a sample **Complaint for Protection from Abuse** in the Appendix. Although you may file a 209A complaint in probate and family, district or superior court, it is preferable to file it in probate court, particularly if there is a divorce action pending, so that all matters may be heard together.

Before you file a "209A", you should consider whether this is the best course for you. **BE AWARE OF THE POSSIBLE CONSEQUENCES OF CALLING THE POLICE OR GOING TO DISTRICT COURT.** Once the wheels of the criminal justice system are set in motion, they may be impossible to stop.

If the police observe signs of physical abuse, or hear an admission, they will arrest your husband regardless of your wishes in the matter. The District Attorney will prosecute your husband for assault and battery, or worse, regardless of your request that this not happen. He may even end up in jail. The D.A.'s office is generally involved in district court 209A actions, but not in probate court 209A actions.

Temporary Custody Order

If your children are living with you and you fear that your husband may try to take them away, you can request a **temporary custody order.** M.G.L. Chapter 208, Section 31 creates a presumption in favor of temporary shared legal custody. This means that it is unlikely, unless your husband is abusive, that you will get full temporary legal and physical custody of your children. In the traditional situation, where the father has been the primary breadwinner and the mother the primary caretaker of the children, the temporary custody order usually provides that both parents share legal custody of the children, with physical custody to the mother.

Shared legal custody means that the parents must consult with each other on all major decisions affecting the children, such as medical care, religious upbringing, education, and extra-curricular activities. The day to day decisions affecting the children will be made by the parent who has **physical custody.**

Sometimes judges award **shared legal and shared physical custody** to each parent. This is rare in a contested situation, as it is confusing and traumatic for the children if their parents are unable to communicate effectively.

The standard which probate judges must use in determining custody issues is **the best interests of the child.** There is no presumption in favor of sharing legal custody at the final hearing. See M.G.L. Chapter 208, Section 31 in the Appendix.

You may choose to file a motion for temporary custody even if the children are living with their father, but most judges will not make a change in physical custody without a full investigation and recommendation by either a **family service officer** of the Probate Court, or a lawyer, psychiatrist, or psychologist who is specially appointed by the court and called a **guardian ad litem.** Generally, except in extreme emergencies, the **status quo** (the way things are) is maintained during the guardian ad litem's investigation.

Violation of a temporary custody order constitutes a criminal offense, namely kidnapping, as well as contempt of court. The enactment of reciprocal child custody laws throughout the United States has significantly reduced the number of cases of children being kidnapped across state lines by non-custodial parents. If you have been awarded custody of your children in Massachusetts, that decision will be honored in other states as well.

In every divorce case involving minor children, it is now necessary to complete a **child custody affidavit**, indicating whether or not custody has been or is being decided elsewhere. See the Appendix.

Temporary Support Order

If your husband will not voluntarily pay a reasonable and adequate amount of support for you and/or the children, you may request a temporary support order. Alimony can be requested at any time during or after a divorce action, so long as you have not waived your right to receive alimony by signing an agreement with your husband before or during the marriage. Child support can be ordered at any time before the child reaches the age of majority, 18, and up to age 23 if the child is domiciled with and principally dependent on you and a full-time student. See the Appendix for the **Child Support Guidelines.**

You must complete and file a **financial statement**, available from the divorce department. You should also obtain a completed financial statement ahead of time from your husband. He is required to provide you with a copy of his financial statement within 10 days of your written request.

If you believe your husband is misrepresenting his income, you may hire a constable to **subpoena** his payroll records from his employer. You should bring copies of the most recent joint income tax returns, paycheck stubs and other proof of income, such as recent bank statements. See the Appendix for the new Rule 410 on Mandatory Self-Disclosure. You have an absolute right to a **mandatory wage assignment**, meaning support payments are deducted from your husband's wages and sent directly to you.

Order to Vacate the Marital Home

If your husband is living at home in a manner that endangers your health, safety, or welfare, or that of your children, you may request that the judge order him to leave. If possible, you should document the real or threatened abuse with **evidence** (such as photographs of damage done, or a doctor's or police report), or bring a **corroborating witness.** If, for example, you can prove your husband is beating you or your children, the judge will order him to leave the home. If the abuse is not physical but is extremely damaging, you may also receive a vacate order. If, however, the abuse consists of no more than occasional shouting, non-violent threats, or other unpleasant behavior, a vacate order will probably not be issued.

You will need to sign an **affidavit,** a notarized sworn statement, describing the events that have caused you to seek the protection of a vacate order. Include the time and place of each event, and focus on the most recent ones.

A vacate order is good for 90 days, but can be renewed. Generally when a person is ordered to leave the house, he does not attempt to return.

Your local police are required to enforce the vacate order. Be sure to have extra copies of the order available as the police will want to keep one for their records. Violation of a vacate order is a criminal offense.

If there is a serious possibility of abuse to you or your children, you might consider leaving your home with the children to stay with friends, relatives, or in a shelter for a few days until you obtain a vacate order. In general, however, it is not advisable to depend on a vacate order to enable you to move back into the house.

Attachment of Real or Personal Property

If you believe that your husband may try to sell real estate or transfer personal property (such as stocks or a savings account), you may make a **motion for an attachment,** specifying a dollar amount that you wish to be attached or "frozen", usually one half the value of the property. You will need to submit an **affidavit** stating that you believe a final judgment of divorce will establish that you are entitled to the property you seek to attach, and that there is a strong likelihood that without the attachment your husband will attempt to convey or conceal it.

If the attachment is granted, you will need to take the judge's order, called the **writ of attachment,** to a sheriff, who will cause it to be recorded properly, i.e., at the Registry of Deeds, if land is involved. The sheriff will charge a fee for this service. Unless there is a restraining order in effect, you are entitled to withdraw funds from a **joint savings account** without any order of the court, although you will have to account for these funds at the divorce hearing.

Attorneys Fees

Supplemental Rule 406 provides for an allowance of attorneys fees and necessary expenses at the beginning of litigation.

Along with the **motion for attorney's fees,** you must submit an **affidavit** that you intend in good faith to prosecute your complaint. Your lawyer submits a **certificate** to the effect that he or she believes your statement to be true, along with a **projected estimate of legal fees, necessary expenses** and the **financial statements** of both parties.

Modification of Temporary Orders

All the temporary orders are in effect "until further order of the court." This means that they will be reviewed and may be altered at a final hearing on your divorce. It also means that you may return to court to get a temporary order modifying a previous temporary order.

DISCOVERY

Discovery is the process of finding out information from the other side regarding finances and other issues relevant to your divorce case. Discovery has been made considerably easier by the recent enactment of Probate Supplemental Rule 410, **Mandatory Self-Disclosure.** Within 45 days of service of the divorce complaint and summons, both parties must exchange tax returns and other listed financial documents as well as health insurance information. See the Appendix for a reprint of Rule 410. If you require additional information, you may discover it in one of the following ways.

Interrogatories are written questions which must be answered by the other side within 30 days. Court permission is required if more than 30 interrogatories or questions are going to be submitted. However, it is possible to submit several sets of less than 30 interrogatories over a period of time, up to the maximum number of 30, before court approval is necessary. If you receive no response to your interrogatories after 30 days, you may go to court and file a **motion to compel discovery,** asking that the court order that your husband answer the interrogatories. Court costs may also be awarded.

You may make a **request for production of documents** requiring your husband to produce financial and other documents relevant to any issue in your case. There is no limit on the number of documents that can be requested, and they must be made available for inspection and copying in 30 days.

It is also possible to request that your husband admit to the truth of certain allegations enumerated by you. This is called a **request for admissions** and must be answered within 30 days. There is no limit on the number of admissions you may ask for.

While interrogatories and requests for admission may be served only on your husband, you may subpoena any witness to attend a **deposition,** to answer any and all questions which are reasonably expected to lead to information that is material and relevant to the issues of the case. There is no limit to the number of questions that can be asked, or the length of time that a deposition may take. A notary public who is also a stenographer takes the oath of the witness and records all of the questions and answers. Subsequently, the stenographer provides a transcript of the deposition, which costs approximately $3.00 per page, to all parties requesting it.

Notice of a deposition must be served on the witness and on your husband at least 7 days before the date of the deposition. A witness may be required to produce documents at the deposition by being served with a **subpoena** listing the documents requested at least 30 days in advance.

A **subpoena** is an order served by a constable or a deputy sheriff directing a person to appear in court or at a deposition to give testimony and/or to bring named documents. A subpoena for appearance or production of documents at a court hearing should be served at least 48 hours before the hearing, and preferably a week or more before, to insure the availability of the witness and to allow the assembly of the documents you are requesting.

If you are representing yourself, you can arrange for subpoenas to be served by contacting a **deputy sheriff** or **constable** directly. They are listed in the Yellow Pages. The fee will include the advance of money which the constable must give to the witness for the witness and travel fee; $35 is an average bill. You may have to pre-pay a deposit.

If you feel that the discovery sought is excessive and/or poses a burden to you, you can request a **protective order** by motion tothe Probate Court. A protective order limits the amount of information that can be requested.

Use at Trial of Discovered Information

Answers to interrogatories, requests for admissions, and questions posed at the deposition of a **party** to the case (you or your husband) can be used at trial to establish the truth of a statement, or for any other purpose, e.g., to show contradiction in statements made in and out of court, or otherwise to impeach the credibility of the other side.

Answers provided at deposition by a witness who is not a party can be used only to attempt to contradict or impeach the testimony of the witness, except if the non-party **deponent** subsequently dies or is genuinely unavailable for trial. In that event, the statements of the non-party witness made at deposition may be used to try to establish the truth of the facts stated.

Often information discovered via interrogatories or deposition leads to the existence of evidence which can later be subpoenaed. Items which are obtained by subpoena, such as payroll records, can be submitted in evidence at trial. It is important that the subpoenaed items be **certified** as true copies of the original record by the person providing them, e.g., the keeper of the payroll records, the bank officer or the Register of Deeds.

TRIAL PREPARATION

First, you must prepare your own **financial statement**. The filing of a current financial statement is required at every hearing on the issue of support. Both parties must file financial statements before a pre-trial or a final hearing can be scheduled. Probate Supplemental Rule 401 entitles you to demand the production of a financial statement within 10 days of making a formal **Request for Financial Statement**. There is also an automatic obligation to exchange financial statements within 45 days of service of a divorce complaint and summons, or at least 2 business days before a hearing. Persons earning $75,000 or more must complete an 8 page financial statement. You may obtain a court order to compel the filing of a financial statement.

You will need to assemble and number the **evidence** that you wish to present, such as tax returns, real estate appraisals, and medical records. Obtain all evidence in the best available form, preferably original or certified copies.

It is also important to decide whether you wish to call any **witnesses**. For example, you might want to subpoena the keeper of the payroll records at your spouse's place of employment, to appear in court with certified records of all wages and benefits paid.

Finally, it will be necessary for you or your attorney to draft a **pre-trial memorandum** or outline of your case for the pre-trial hearing.

THE PRE-TRIAL HEARING

The pre-trial is an effort by the court to assist you and your husband to settle the case, or in the alternative, to determine the issues which are con-tested. Approximately 80% of all cases which go to pre-trial are settled.

The preparation for a pre-trial hearing is essentially identical to pre-paration for a final hearing. If possible, **discovery** should be completed prior to the pre-trial. The **evidence** should be assembled in its best available form, e.g., certified copies of payroll records, bank statements, deeds, and so forth. You must also list the names of the persons you expect to call as **witnesses**. Current **financial statements** must be filed by both parties.

The above information is included in your **pre-trial memorandum**, a 5 to 10 page summary of your case, following the format required by the **pre-trial notice and order** of the court. See the Appendix.

At the pre-trial hearing, the judge may first meet alone with the lawyers, to read the pre-trial memoranda of both parties and inquire as to the possibility of a settlement. The judge may suggest a compromise and ask the attorneys to discuss it with their clients.

The judge may then invite both parties and their attorneys to meet **in chambers** to discuss a settlement of the case, pointing out the benefits of reaching an agreement, as opposed to proceeding with a trial. Some judges prefer to conduct pre-trial conferences in open court. Pre-trial conferences must be tape recorded, as are all other hearings.

If it appears that the parties are willing to reach an agreement, the judge will encourage them to keep talking until they succeed. A **family service officer** may assist. An agreement is often arrived at in this manner and put in writing on the day of the pre-trial. The handwritten agreement, signed by both husband and wife and by their lawyers, is presented to the judge for approval. The judge then hears the case as an uncontested divorce, and the matter is concluded, to the relief of all.

If it appears that no agreement is possible, the judge will set a date for a **trial**. As the pre-trial notice indicates, the judge may also proceed with a **trial** on the date of the pre-trial although this rarely happens.

Most judges abhor this practice because of the undue pressure to settle and the unfair agreement which is likely to result. Your lawyer may know if the pre-trial judge is likely to use the threat of immediate trial to force a settlement, and might file a motion for a continuance of any possible trial, upon receipt of the pre-trial notice. Or you may call the judge's clerk to ask whether there is any chance that the judge will start a trial on the day of the pre-trial. If so, you may file a **motion for a continuance of the trial**, stating the reasons why you would not be ready to start a trial on the day of the pre-trial and/or why you would be at a disadvantage at the pre-trial if you were negotiating under threat of a trial to begin that day, in the event that you and your husband were unable to reach an agreement.

THE TRIAL

The trial is your day in court, and may in fact take several days. It is difficult to represent yourself at trial. If possible, you should be retain a competent, experienced family lawyer.

If you must represent yourself, stick to the facts. Don't waste time on insignificant details. Support your statements with documentary evidence, or with the corroborating testimony of witnesses, when possible. Do not draw conclusions or make judgments about the facts. That is the judge's job.

You will need to testify concerning your grounds for divorce. In a no-fault divorce, a brief statement that your marriage is over is sufficient. See Chapter 8 for the elements of the 7 fault grounds for divorce. You should be thoroughly familiar with M.G.L. Chapter 208, Section 34, which is in the Appendix, and offer testimony and/or evidence on each of the factors listed. If custody of minor children is an issue, see Chapter 9.

If you are the **plaintiff**, you will present your case first. Your lawyer will ask you questions on **direct examination.** If you do not know the answer to the question, say so. Otherwise, answer the question to the best of your ability, but do not offer information that is not requested. When your lawyer has concluded, he or she will state, "I have no further questions of this witness, your honor." You then remain on the stand for **cross-examination** by your husband's attorney. Your lawyer may then wish to ask you some questions on **re-direct**, to clear up any confusion or wrong impression created by the cross-examination. This procedure is followed for each witness called by your lawyer. Then he or she will say, "I rest my case," and your husband's lawyer will call a succession of witnesses in the same manner.

If your lawyer or your husband's lawyer raises an objection to a question being asked, by standing and saying, **"I object,"** you should wait until the judge rules on the objection before answering. **"Over-ruled"** means you can answer the question because the judge does not agree that there is a valid objection to it. **"Sustained"** means you cannot answer the question, as the judge has decided that the objection to it is valid. There are many reasons for objection, including asking a leading question of a witness on direct examination, asking an immaterial or irrelevant question, asking a question about documentary evidence that has not been properly introduced, and asking a question that calls for a conclusion or hearsay.

If you are representing yourself, you will be making direct statements to the judge, who may also question you directly. Then you will be cross-examined by your husband's attorney. It is enormously difficult to be both your own witness and your own attorney. Your lack of familiarity with the law and with the rules of procedure and evidence will not help matters.

The Judgment

After you, your husband, and your witnesses, if any, have completed your testimony, the hearing is over and you will have to wait several days or weeks until the judge's decision arrives in the mail.

The judge will ask both lawyers to prepare **suggested findings of fact and rulings of law,** summarizing the relevant facts and the law in your case, also to draft suggested orders. A **suggested order** spells out what you and your lawyer are asking the judge to order in your case.

A **judgment of divorce nisi** (conditional) will be entered on or after the last day of your final hearing, and sent to you or your lawyer. Your divorce judgment will become final 90 days after the date of the **judgment nisi,** with no further notice to you.

You may arrange for a **stenographer** to record the testimony in a contested case. You then order a **transcript,** a typed record of the testimony, certified by the stenographer, who is also a notary public. The cost is approximately $3.00 per triple-spaced page, which means hundreds of dollars for several hours. The **certified transcript** can then be used in a later legal proceeding, including an appeal or any post-trial motions.

All hearings, including hearings on temporary orders, are now required to be tape-recorded by the court. You are then entitled to purchase a copy of the tape at $37.50 each. Unfortunately, it takes 4 to 6 weeks to obtain an official copy of the tape recordings. For some strange reason, they are shipped to Springfield and back, rather than duplicated on site.

Statement of Objections

At any time before the divorce judgment has become final, you may file a **statement of objections** with the probate court, listing the reasons why you object to the divorce judgment becoming final, such as the discovery of new evidence which you could not have found before the trial, or the discovery of fraud on your husband's part. For example, you learned after the hearing that your husband had excluded certain assets or income from his financial statement. In this event, he may also be found guilty of perjury, for which the court may impose penalties. The court will schedule a hearing on your statement of objections, and the divorce will not become final until the matter is disposed of. There is no filing fee.

Appeal

You do have the option to appeal a judgment with which you are dissatisfied. However, an appellate court will reverse a probate court decision only if a **clear abuse of judicial discretion** resulting in **harmful error** is apparent on the record of your case. This is very difficult to prove, as probate judges have broad discretion in determining custody, visitation, property division, support, and other issues involved in divorce.

A **claim and notice of appeal** must be filed in the probate court within 30 days of the entry of the judgment. The Register of Probate has 40 days in which to assemble a record of your case and will notify the parties when this has been done. The **record on appeal** consists of all pleadings filed with the court, and any exhibits admitted in evidence. A certified **transcript** of the testimony is also part of the record on appeal, and is made from the stenographer's notes or from the tapes.

Your claim of appeal must be filed with the Clerk of the **Appeals Court,** Suffolk County Court House, Room 1500, Boston, Massachusetts 02108, (617) 725-8106, within 10 days thereafter, along with a $150 filing fee, which will be waived if you are indigent. A docket number will be assigned to the case, and your lawyer will be given 40 days in which to file an appellate brief on the facts and the law. Your husband's lawyer will file a brief in response within the next 30 days.

About 4 to 6 months after the briefs have been filed, the case will be scheduled for oral argument. Alternatively, the Appeals Court may make a decision without allowing the opportunity for oral argument. The Appeals Court will generally render a decision within 3 months of the oral argument.

It is also possible to appeal a temporary (interlocutory) order, but not advisable as the Appeals Court will not reverse a temporary order of the probate court, except on a showing of both abuse of judicial discretion resulting in prejudicial error and the existence of an emergency or threat of irreparable harm requiring the immediate intervention of a single justice of the Appeals Court. The fee for such an appeal to a single justice is $160.

If you do decide to appeal, a lawyer is essential, at least to consult with. He or she will need to research the law and legal precedents on the issues in your case, and present well-reasoned arguments supporting a reversal of the probate judgment.

If you win the appeal, you may return to the probate court for a judgment in accordance with the appellate decision. Otherwise, the judgment of the probate court is affirmed.

It is important to note that, unless you are also appealing that portion of the **divorce judgment nisi** which dissolved the marriage, the divorce itself will become final 90 days after the entry of the divorce judgment nisi. All other provisions of the judgment remain in effect unless a **stay** is granted by the probate judge or by a single justice of the Appeals Court. Application for a stay must be made to the probate judge first.

Chapter 9   THE CONTESTED CUSTODY CASE

The first thing to understand about the contested custody case is that it is to be avoided if at all possible. The trauma to both parents and children of a battle over custody is incalculable. The scars are often life long. If you and your husband really love your children, you will work out a mutually satisfactory custody arrangement with the assistance of lawyers, therapists, advisors, mutual friends, or mediators.

Divorce is almost always a devastating experience for children. Your child needs to be reassured that he or she is still loved by both parents, even though they may have stopped loving each other. Most children wish desperately that their parents would get back together, regardless of the problems that may have existed. They are best able to cope with their parents' divorce when their parents are able to communicate constructively.

A contested custody case is a very lengthy and involved proceeding, and it is essential that you be represented by an experienced family lawyer. If you cannot afford a lawyer, the judge may order your husband to pay your legal fees, after a hearing on your motion. See Chapter 8.

Court Appointed Investigator

The judge will appoint a specialist to investigate the custody situation and will generally follow his or her recommendation. The custody specialist appointed by the judge may be either a **family service officer** from the court, or an attorney, psychiatrist or psychologist, who is called a **guardian ad litem**, "g.a.l." for short.

The family service office often is unable because of insufficient staffing to undertake an investigation and report. When a **g.a.l.** is appointed to do the job, he or she may charge as much as $150 per hour and take up to a year to complete an investigation and file a report.

The court appointed investigator will meet several times with you, with your husband, and with your children to evaluate the respective home situations. He or she may also meet with your child's teacher, physician, therapist, babysitter, relatives, and neighbors. You should provide the investigator with a list of names, addresses, and telephone numbers of people who are familiar with your child, your home situation, and your parenting abilities.

At the conclusion of the investigation, the **family service officer** or **g.a.l.** files a **report** with the court which summarizes the findings and recommends a plan for the children. You will be notified that the report has been filed and that you may go to the courthouse and read the report and take notes on it, but you may not obtain a copy unless a judge allows your motion for it. Your attorney may decide to challenge the report and may subpoena and cross-examine the investigator in an effort to challenge the findings and recommendations. This is rarely successful, since the investigator was appointed by the judge, who is sure to have confidence in his or her competence and impartiality.

Psychiatric Evaluations

You may request that the court order a psychiatric evaluation of your husband or you may subpoena a psychiatrist who has treated your husband, and require him or her to testify as to your husband's mental health and parenting history. Your husband will almost certainly respond in kind.

It is important to note that in a contested custody proceeding, the patient-psychiatrist privilege is waived. This means that your psychiatrist must give the court any information that is relevant to the issue of custody, particularly your fitness as a parent. Even though discussions between a patient and a psychiatrist are generally confidential, this is not the case in a contested custody hearing.

The Standard For Determining Custody

The standard which probate judges must use in determining custody is **the best interests of the child.** The determining factor is the happiness and welfare of the child. The law states that the rights of parents shall, in the absence of misconduct, be equal.

It is widely believed that a minimum of change and upheaval is best for children. It is rare for a judge to order a child who has been living with one parent to change homes, unless the child is being abused or neglected.

It sometimes happens that the investigation reveals both parents to be unfit, and the court has the power to order that a third party, such as a grandparent or aunt, have temporary custody of the child. If no relative is willing or able to care for the child, custody may be given to the Department of Social Services, and the child placed in a foster home. This happens extremely infrequently, and only when the court is convinced that the child is at risk with either parent, as, for example, when both parents are severely alcoholic and abusive to the child.

If you have been the primary caretaker of your child up to the time of the hearing, there is a strong likelihood that you will be awarded physical custody of the child. It is important to present evidence of parental responsibilities that you have consistently undertaken, such as dental and medical appointments, meetings with teachers and involvement with your child's afterschool activities, as well as the day to day care of your child.

The Custody Decision

Massachusetts General Laws, chapter 208, section 31 creates a presumption in favor of **temporary shared legal custody.** There is no such presumption at the final hearing. However, the temporary custody arrangement sets a powerful precedent. Most parents who divorce continue to share in the major decisions concerning the child, such as schooling, religious education, medical care, vacations, camp, etc. and have **shared** or **joint legal custody.** However, it is still common for just one parent to have **physical custody** of the child. The parent who has physical custody provides the primary home, and the non-custodial parent generally has the right to visit at all reasonable times, or pursuant to a schedule or **parenting plan.**

A judge may also award **shared physical custody** to parents, although this rarely occurs. In this situation, the child is considered to have two homes, and often spends an equal amount of time with each parent. Recent studies have shown that children do better when they have a stable home base and a minimum of transitions, back and forth between homes.

You might try to work out a shared custody arrangement, instead of going through the enormous expense and trauma of a contested custody case.

Visits

The non-custodial parent (the parent who does not have physical custody) is generally given the right of reasonable visitation with the children. If, however, you and your husband have not been able to agree on visits and/or have a history of arguments on this subject, the judge may order a visit schedule, such as every other weekend and one evening during the week.

The right to visit may be suspended in extreme situations, such as those involving physical or sexual abuse. It is routinely suspended when a 209A order is first issued, for a few days until the second hearing when your husband will also be present in court to be heard on this issue.

You are in contempt of court if you interfere with your husband's right to visit the children. However, he is not in contempt if he does not exercise his right to visit. Your children are, of course, the losers in any dispute over visits. See the Appendix for a reprint of the Massachusetts Bar Foundation's pamphlet **Parents After Separation—Guidelines For Visitation.**

Child Support

At the same time that the judge makes a decision on custody, he or she will also determine the amount of support to be paid by the non-custodial parent. In most cases, the judge is required to follow the **child support guidelines** in determining the amount of child support to be paid. See the Appendix. Money is not a factor in awarding custody, and you are not at a disadvantage if your earnings are substantially less than your husband's.

Medical Insurance

The judge's order will include a provision for medical insurance for the children. If your husband's employer is providing coverage, your husband will be ordered to exercise the option of additional coverage for the children and for you. If there is an incremental cost for your future coverage, you will most likely be required to pay it.

The Family Home

In order to minimize the disruption to the children, and also because it usually makes financial sense in today's housing market, the judge will most likely allow the custodial parent to remain in the jointly owned home with the children until the youngest has graduated from high school. The house is then sold and the net proceeds are divided between the husband and wife pursuant to the judge's order, often in a 50/50 split.

Chapter 10   ENFORCEMENT OF YOUR DIVORCE JUDGMENT

If your husband is violating the terms of your judgment of divorce, separate support, or modification, you can return to probate court for enforcement.

You will need to file a **complaint for contempt** which describes the violation in question, such as non-payment of support. A sample complaint is included in the Appendix. There is no filing fee.

The court will issue a **contempt summons** and this must be served on your husband either (1) in person by a sheriff or constable or (2) by leaving a copy of the complaint and summons at his last known address, while at the same time mailing a copy to him by certified mail. Keep the returned certified mail receipt for proof of service. It is also possible for your husband to accept service of the contempt summons, although he is unlikely to do so.

The contempt summons will include the date and time of the hearing on your complaint. Your husband must appear in court at that time. If he fails to do so, a **default judgment** may be entered against him. Alternatively a **capias** or **bench warrant** may be issued for his arrest.

Your husband must be served with a copy of the complaint and summons at least 7 days before the hearing date. He may file an **answer** to your complaint, indicating that he intends to contest it, at any time during this 7 day period. If you are unable to serve your husband on time, you must return the contempt summons to the probate court and ask that it be reissued with a new date.

Support

If support is at issue, both you and your husband will be required to file current **financial statements** with the court before the hearing.

At the hearing, your husband will have to explain why he has not fulfilled **his child support** or alimony obligations. The **burden of proof** is on him to show that he did not violate the judgment, or that there was a good reason for the violation, e.g., he lost his job. If he can show that through no fault of his own he is unable to make the payments, then the judge can **modify** the support obligation.

If your husband is found to be in contempt of court for violation of a support order, he will be ordered to pay what he owes, either in a lump sum or in instalments. However, you should not wait until there is a huge arrearage in support before you seek enforcement of the divorce judgment. There is a possibility that the judge may reduce or "forgive" part of the support arrears because of problems of proof or because of your husband's inability to pay.

You do have an absolute right to a **mandatory wage assignment** or a **pension assignment** requiring your husband's employer to deduct support from his paycheck or pension and mail it directly to you, or to the Department of Revenue ("D.O.R."), which will then forward it to you.

The probate court may also **attach** the real estate, bank account, or other property of your husband in order to satisfy an unpaid support obligation.

Federal and state **tax refunds** due to your husband may be intercepted by the D.O.R. and applied against the support arrears. Numerous other sanctions, such as forfeiture of professional or driver's licenses or even jail are available, although invoked only in the most extreme cases after all other attempts to collect child support have failed.

If your husband has wilfully quit his job or has refused to seek employment, the court may also issue a **work order**, requiring him to submit weekly proof of 5 to 10 job applications to a **family service officer.**

Visits

Most contempt actions are brought because of non-payment of support. A parent may also be found in contempt of court for refusing to allow visits with minor children in violation of a court order. It is not, however, possible to force a parent to visit his or her children. A court-ordered visit would not be a good experience for the child.

It is never a good idea to deny visitation because of non-payment of support. It is very bad for children to be denied access to either parent at any time and especially to be also caught up in their parents' conflict over money.

If you are having problems with visits, seek the assistance of a counselor or mutual friend before returning to court. The Massachusetts Bar Foundation has prepared a helpful list of visit guidelines. See Appendix.

Custody

If your husband has violated the custody provisions of your divorce judgment by, for example, kidnapping your minor children after the court awarded you physical custody, you should contact your local police and the F.B.I. immediately. They will help you locate your children without any further order of the court.

In recent years, the adoption of the **Uniform Child Custody Act** by every state in the union has significantly reduced the incidence of kidnapping by non-custodial parents. Each state honors the custody order which has already been issued by another state. A **child custody affidavit,** stating whether another court has adjudicated the issue of custody, must be filed in every action involving minor children. See Appendix. Thus, it is no longer possible for a parent to try to obtain custody in another state if a custody decision has already been made, or if a court has assumed **jurisdiction** (power to decide) in a custody matter.

It is a criminal offense to violate a child custody order or a restraining order. A **jail sentence** may be imposed.

Property Settlement

If your husband is refusing to fulfill his obligation to convey real estate, securities or other property, most of the sanctions described in the support section above are available.

In addition, the judge may order a third party, such as a bank or trustee, to convey property to you. Real estate may be conveyed by order of the court, which is then recorded in the Registry of Deeds.

Attorney's Fees

If your husband is found to be in contempt, he will also be ordered to pay your attorney's fees for bringing the contempt action. You should request this on the complaint or by motion. Although attorney's fees are rarely awarded in other matters, they are generally included in a judgment of contempt.

Out of State Support Enforcement

If your husband has moved out of state, you will be going to your local district court rather than the probate court to enforce the support provisions of your judgment.

The clerk will help you to complete a complaint under the provisions of the **Uniform Reciprocal Enforcement of Support Act.** Be sure to bring with you a certified copy of the divorce judgment. A list of district courts is provided in the Appendix.

The district court will contact a court in your husband's state and it will arrange service of the U.R.E.S.A. complaint and summons on him. Your husband will be required to appear in court in his state and explain why there has been a problem with payment of support. If he has a valid excuse, the support payments may be modified by the out of state court.

This procedure does take several months. However, there will most likely be a **mandatory wage assignment**, and you will then not have a repeat of the non-support problem, so long as he remains employed.

If your divorce judgment was granted in another state, a probate court in Massachusetts has the power to enforce the support provisions.

Enforcement of Foreign Judgments

The new Rule 56 on **summary judgment** is available to modify or enforce a foreign judgment, if there is no real dispute as to the material facts. See Chapter 11 for a description of the **summary judgment** procedure.

Chapter 11   MODIFICATION OF YOUR DIVORCE JUDGMENT

Modification of Massachusetts Judgments

At any time after the judgment of divorce has been issued, you may return to probate court to request that the provisions be changed.

The probate and family court retains jurisdiction to modify provisions relating to children, up to age 18 for custody and visit issues, and up to age 23 for child support and education issues, for full-time students.

If you and your husband executed a separation agreement which by its own terms **survives the divorce judgment as an independent contract,** you will not succeed in altering the spousal support provisions, except if you might otherwise become a **public charge,** i.e. you are eligible for welfare benefits.

If your separation agreement is **merged in the divorce judgment,** then the court will be able to change the support provisions once you have shown a material change of circumstances. See Chapter 7.

Property settlements are not subject to modification, except where fraud is proven. For example, your husband did not disclose to you his ownership of real estate or other property at the time of your divorce.

You will have to file a **complaint for modification** describing the relevant changes that have occurred, and the order that you are seeking. See Appendix. There is a $111.00 filing fee. If the complaint relates to support or education of a child, there is no filing fee. You will, however, have to pay $1.00 for the summons, which you will receive in about a week by mail, unless you file your complaint in person.

The **complaint for modification** and **summons** must be served on your husband by a sheriff or constable, or your husband may accept service by signing the original summons before a notary public.

You then return the original summons to the court. You must wait 20 days after your husband has been served before you can request a hearing. This allows him to file an **answer** to your complaint, if he wishes. Use the trial request form shown in the Appendix at any time after the 20 days have gone by, and send a copy to your husband.

At the hearing, the **burden of proof** will be on you to show that a **material change of circumstances** has occurred. For example, your husband may now be earning substantially more money and support payments based on his previous salary may be inadequate, or your income may have decreased substantially. Unemployment and disability are often cited as reasons for seeking a modification.

In addition to modification of a support order, it is possible to request a change in the custody or visit provisions. The process is similar to that involved in a contested custody case and a guardian ad litem is often appointed to investigate and report to the court. It is difficult to obtain a modification of custody provisions, however, because judges are reluctant to

48

change the living arrangements of the children, except where it is clearly in their best interests. See Chapter 9 for more information on contested custody cases.

Child Support Guidelines

The **Child Support Guidelines** are now routinely applied in actions for modification. Along with the complaint and summons, you should serve your former husband with a **motion for temporary child support pursuant to the guidelines** following the motion procedure described in Chapter 8.

At the motions hearing, which takes place two weeks or more after service, depending on the backlog of cases in your county, each of you must file an updated financial statement and related documents required by the new Supplemental Rule 410 on Mandatory Self-Disclosure, included in the Appendix. A family service officer will use this information to compute child support pursuant to the guidelines. Generally a Stipulation is then signed by the parties, and the new child support amount is implemented by wage assignment. In most instances, this will be the end of the case.

Removal of Children from Massachusetts

Even if you have full custody of your children, you may not relocate with them to another state or country without the consent of their father.

However, the court may allow such a move if you have a "good, sincere reason" and you can show that it would be a "real advantage" for you and the children. The usual reasons given are remarriage and better employment.

If possible, try to reach an agreement with your former husband, because it may take many months for the court to reach a decision. It is customary to make some concessions on child support, in consideration of travel expenses. Also, the visit schedule is often changed to include most of the summer and school vacations.

Modification of Out of State Divorce Judgments

The probate court may modify a divorce judgment made by a court in another state, but special rules apply. If the defendant has been properly served with the modification complaint and summons, the probate court has **personal jurisdiction**, and may modify in any way a foreign judgment that was entered **without personal jurisdiction over both parties**, i.e., the **defendant** was not properly served in the original divorce action.

If the foreign court **did have personal jurisdiction over both parties** (i.e. personal service was properly made on the **defendant**), a Massachusetts probate court can modify the out of state judgment only to the extent that it is modifiable under the laws of the foreign court. For example, if you signed a waiver of alimony in your Iowa divorce, making it impossible for an Iowa court to make a future alimony award, then a Massachusetts probate court will not be able to award alimony either.

However, **if both you and your husband are now** living in **Massachusetts,** then the probate court can modify any provision of the foreign judgment, except a property division which was made by a foreign court having personal jurisdiction of both parties. Again, personal jurisdiction over a **defendant** arises only after a defendant has been properly served. A **plaintiff** submits to a court's jurisdiction by filing the complaint.

Modification Pursuant to Other Complaint

Probate judges have broad **equity** powers. They can take action on their own to do what is just and equitable, regardless of the **pleadings,** which are the claims and answers filed by the parties.

There is always the possibility, when bringing an action in court, that one or both parties will be unpleasantly surprised at the result. This is one reason why it makes sense to settle, rather than litigate, whenever possible.

A judge may modify the provisions of a prior order or of an agreement that has been **merged** in a judgment of divorce and will do so if a significant change of circumstance has occurred. For example, it sometimes happens that a probate judge modify the provisions of an existing judgment at a hearing on a **complaint for contempt** even though no **complaint for modification** was filed.

Summary Judgment

As of December 1, 1997, there is a new **Rule 56 SUMMARY JUDGMENT** which has been added to the Rules of Domestic Relations Procedure. It allows the filing of a **Motion for Summary Judgment** in actions for modification and in actions to modify or enforce a foreign divorce judgment only.

The basis for this motion is the assertion that there is no genuine issue as to any material fact. For example, your motion for summary judgment might state that even if everything your former husband alleges in his **Complaint for Modification** is true, you maintain that you should not have a decrease in support as a matter of law, because you and he made a binding separation agreement which survived as an independent contract.

Every motion for summary judgment must be accompanied by an **Affidavit of Undisputed Facts.** In the above example, your affidavit will spell out in numbered paragraphs the facts you rely upon in support of your motion and will contain a reference to and a copy of the appropriate provisions of your separation agreement.

The opposing party is required to admit those facts which are undisputed and deny those which are disputed in the Affidavit of Undisputed Facts. He or she may file an **Affidavit of Disputed Facts** enumerating additional facts which raise a genuine issue which ought to be tried.

This new rule should be an effective way to quickly dispose of very straightforward cases, such as those seeking modification of child support amounts based on the guidelines.

Chapter 12　LEGAL RIGHTS OF MARRIED WOMEN IN MASSACHUSETTS

The Right to Make a Contract

A married woman may contract with third parties independently of her husband. She may also make a contract with her husband, either before, during or after marriage, and the contract will be enforceable in court. It is not uncommon for people entering a second marriage to make a **pre-marriage contract** or **antenuptial agreement** which defines their financial rights and responsibilities during the marriage, and in the event of divorce.

As with any contract, it is imperative that you consult a competent attorney before you sign. After you sign, you will be bound by the provisions of the contract regardless of whether you had sufficient legal advice, unless you can prove **fraud** or **duress** (coercion).

It is preferable that the contract be drafted by a lawyer and that the signatures of both parties be notarized.

The Right to Her Own Credit

A married woman has the right to establish credit in her own name based on her own income. It is illegal to deny credit on the basis of sex or marital status. If a married woman is without a sufficient source of independent income, she will however be denied credit in her own name.

A married woman who has a joint credit account with her husband is entitled to have the benefit of the credit history on the account. The fact that the bills have been paid on time on the joint account will enable her to show that she is a good credit risk when in the future she applies for her own credit.

The Right to Own Property

A married woman has the right to own property as an individual, or jointly with her husband and/or with third parties.

Real estate is most often owned by husband and wife as **tenants by the entirety**, a form of joint ownership that can only be used by married couples and which grants special protection against creditors, except on joint obligations. When one spouse dies, the survivor owns the real estate. Upon final judgment of divorce, if no other disposition has been made, the ownership of the real estate changes automatically to a **tenancy in common:** each party holds a one half share which can be sold or willed to a third party without the consent of the other owner. At the death of one tenant in common, the other retains only his or her one half share, not the entire real estate.

A third form of joint ownership recognized in Massachusetts is the **joint tenancy.** Unlike the tenancy by the entirety, its use is not limited to married couples and it affords no protection against creditors. Like tenancy by the entirety, each owner has an equal interest in the whole property and, in the event of the death of one joint tenant, the survivor owns the real estate outright. Most joint bank accounts are joint tenancies.

The Right to Sue and Be Sued

A married woman may sue and be sued in contract or in **tort** (a wrongful act not involving a breach of contract) as if she were single. She is not liable for her husband's individual debts, except that she is jointly liable with her husband for up to $100 on each bill incurred for necessaries furnished with her knowledge or consent, if she has property of $2,000 or more.

The Right to Inherit From Her Spouse

Unless she waives her inheritance rights in a contract with her husband, or a probate court has entered a judgment pursuant to Massachusetts General Laws, chapter 209, section 36 that she has deserted her husband or he is living apart from her for justifiable cause, a widow in Massachusetts is entitled to a share of her husband's estate whether or not he provides for her in his will.

When There is No Will

If her husband dies without leaving a will, and is survived by blood relatives but there are no children, a widow is entitled to the entire net probate estate if its value does not exceed $200,000. Otherwise, the widow takes $200,000 and one half the remaining estate. The decedent's relatives receive the rest pursuant to M.G.L., Chapter 190, Section 3.

If her husband dies without leaving a will and there are children, the widow takes one half the net probate estate. The children receive the rest in equal shares. The **net probate estate** is the real and personal property remaining after the debts of the decedent, his funeral expenses, and the estate taxes have been paid.

If her husband dies without leaving a will and there are no surviving children or blood relatives, then the widow takes the whole net probate estate.

When There is a Will

If her husband dies leaving a will which makes little or no provision for her, a widow has the right to waive the will and demand a forced share of his estate.

If the deceased left blood relatives but no children, the widow takes $25,000 outright, plus one half the remaining net probate estate of which she receives the first $25,000 outright and the balance as a life estate. A **life estate** gives her the right to use the property and to spend any income from it during her life: real estate is hers for life but she cannot sell or mortgage it, and personal property (e.g., a bank account) is held in trust.

If the deceased left children, the widow's forced share is one third of the net probate estate, with $25,000 received outright and a life estate in the remainder. If the deceased left no children and no blood relatives, the widow takes $25,000 and one half the remaining net probate estate, of which she receives the first $25,000 outright and the balance as a **life estate.**

For example, in an estate worth $225,000 after payment of the decedent's debts and taxes, the widow in this instance will receive $50,000 outright and a life estate in $75,000 worth of real and/or personal property.

After the surviving spouse has received his or her forced share, the remainder of the net probate estate is disposed of in accordance with the provisions of the will, with a proportionate reduction in the share of each beneficiary.

Revocation of a Will by Marriage or Divorce

Marriage revokes a will made by a person previous to the marriage, unless the will states that it was made in contemplation of marriage. If a person dies without making a new will after the marriage, it is as if he or she died without making a will.

A final judgment of divorce or annulment revokes any disposition of property made by will to a former spouse or the appointment of the former spouse as executor, trustee, conservator or guardian, unless the will expressly provides otherwise. Provisions revoked in this manner by divorce or annulment are revived upon remarriage to the former spouse.

The Right to Receive Support

A married woman has the right to receive **alimony** from her husband if she is without sufficient means to support herself, and he has the ability to make a financial contribution. She also has the right to receive **child support** and **education expenses** for her dependent children up to age 23. See the Appendix for the **Child Support Guidelines.** In order to obtain an order for alimony or child support, a complaint for divorce or for separate support must be filed in the probate court. A district court may also issue an order for temporary support pursuant to family abuse prevention action. A later order of the probate court will supersede the district court order.

Support orders now routinely include a **mandatory wage assignment** directing the employer to withhold support from the payor's paycheck and forward it to the court, or directly to you the payee. You may, if you wish, sign a waiver of your right to a wage assignment, but you are, of course, giving up a degree of financial security if you do.

The Right to Medical Insurance Coverage

A married woman has the right to be included in her husband's medical insurance coverage, if she does not have her own insurance, and vice versa. The coverage must also be extended to the minor children of the marriage.

The Right to Social Security Benefits Based on Her Husband's Earnings

If the marriage lasted 10 years or more, a wife is entitled to receive Social Security benefits based on her former husband's earnings. At least two years must have elapsed since the divorce before benefits can be collected. The wife must be at least 62 before she can start collecting and will, at that age, receive a benefit equal to $37\frac{1}{2}\%$ of the husband's benefit.

If she waits until age 65, she will receive the maximum benefit of 50% of the husband's entitlement. For further details, call the Social Security Administration, (800) 772-1213.

The Right to Share Pension

A married person has a right to one half of all pension benefits accumulated during the marriage by the other spouse.

The Right to Protection from Abuse

A married woman has the right to protection from physical abuse by her husband. Protective restraining and vacate orders against an abusive husband or other household member may be obtained from the district court or the probate court pursuant to a complaint for family abuse prevention, Massachusetts General Laws, Chapter 209A. See Chapter 2.

Restraining and vacate orders may also be issued by the probate court pursuant to a complaint for divorce or separate support. The violation of restraining and vacate orders is a criminal offense.

However, you should be warned that if you seek the help of the police and or the district courts, they may insist on proceeding with criminal charges against your husband even though you don't want this. Although you cannot be forced to testify against your husband, you may not be able to prevent his criminal prosecution for battery, for example.

Over-eager assistant district attorneys often fail to respect a woman's wish to maintain her marriage and forgive an incident of abuse. This is an over-reaction by the system which should be corrected in the interest of family preservation and because it will keep women from seeking help when it is needed.

The Right to Keep or Change Her Name

A married woman has the right to keep her own name after marriage, or to return to it at any time. Anyone can change her name in any way at any time, for any honest purpose, without a court order. This is called a **common law name change.**

However, a name change is generally confirmed by **probate court order**, as this eliminates any potential hassles with a business or government agency which may question the use of a new name. A court order for a change of name can be obtained at the time of a **final hearing on divorce**, by requesting it on the divorce complaint or by a subsequent motion. There is no additional fee and you do not need to file a copy of your birth certificate with the court.

Otherwise, a court order may be obtained by filing a **petition for a name change.** The filing fee is $60, and you must file a copy of your birth certificate in this separate name change action.

Chapter 13   TAX CONSEQUENCES OF DIVORCE

It is important to consider the tax consequences of the financial provisions of your separation agreement or court order.

The following is a brief overview of some of the tax issues common to
divorce. Because the tax laws are complex and constantly changing, it is a
good idea for you to consult an accountant, financial advisor, or tax attorney
before you sign your separation agreement, or participate in a pre-trial
hearing. You may obtain free information from the Internal Revenue Service,
J.F.K. Federal Building, Boston MA 02205, 1-800-829-1040 and from the
Massachusetts Department of Revenue, 100 Cambridge Street, Boston MA 02204,
1-800-392-6089.

Alimony vs. Child Support

Alimony received by you is taxable income and must be included on
your state and federal tax returns. Your husband will be able to deduct the
alimony amount he pays you from his income, and must provide your social security number on his return. The alimony must be paid pursuant to a signed separation agreement or a court order. Voluntary payments are not deductible by
him or taxable to you.

The **child support** you receive is not taxable income, and you do not
include it on your return. Your husband does not get a deduction for the
child support which he pays.

A court order or separation agreement made before **December 31, 1984,**
which provides for **an unallocated amount of alimony and child support,** is
regarded as alimony. The entire amount is taxable to you and deductible by
your husband.

Changes in the tax law **effective January 1, 1985,** make it more difficult to designate a support amount as alimony, rather than child support.
The following rules apply to all separation agreements and support orders
made after January 1, 1985.

The payment of **alimony cannot be conditioned on an event related to the
support of a child,** such as the child's reaching a specified age, graduat-
ing from school, leaving home, or marrying. Even if such a contingency is
not stated in the support provisions of your divorce judgment or agreement,
the IRS will disallow all or part of the alimony designation if the payments
end or are reduced when the obligation to pay support for the child ends.
For example, "alimony" payments end on a named date, which happens to be
within 6 months of your youngest child's 18th birthday.

The divorce judgment or agreement must state that the **alimony ends on
the death of the recipient.**

If a **temporary support order** states that the support amount (or a
designated part of it) is alimony, then the IRS will honor the order,
regardless of the length of time it remains in effect, or the amount paid.

Husband and wife may agree that the spousal support being paid is not taxable to her as alimony and the IRS will honor the **agreement,** a copy of which must be attached to the wife's tax return. The husband would then not be able to take a tax deduction for the support paid.

Only **cash payments** (cash, check or money order) can qualify as alimony. The transfer of real or personal property, such as a house or stocks, cannot qualify as alimony. Cash payments to a third party, such as rent, mortgage, or tuition, can qualify as alimony, if required by agreement or court order.

Lump Sum Cash Payments

A **lump sum cash payment** made by your husband to you is not taxable to you or deductible by him, even if your agreement states that it is made in consideration of your agreement to waive your right to alimony.

You and your husband may, however, agree to call up to $15,000 of the lump sum cash settlement **alimony,** in any one year. You would pay income tax only on the amount designated as alimony.

A lump sum payment of **alimony arrears** is always considered alimony. However, a **voluntary lump sum prepayment** does not qualify as alimony. In order for a payment to qualify as alimony, there must be a present obligation to pay established by a separation agreement or court order.

A lump sum cash settlement, paid in annual installments pursuant to the terms of a separation agreement or final judgment of divorce made prior to 1985, must be paid in a period of less than 10 years, or it is considered alimony. Even if the installments are payable in less than 10 years but will stop upon the happening of a contingency such as death or remarriage, they are taxable as alimony. However, no more than 10% of the total cash settlement is deemed alimony in any one year.

Conveyance of Jointly Owned Real Estate

Prior to July 19, 1984, a transfer of one spouse's interest in jointly owned real estate to the other spouse was considered a taxable event, when made pursuant to a separation agreement or judgment of divorce. For example, when a husband conveyed his share of the house to his wife (by a deed from husband and wife to wife alone), he had to pay a capital gains tax as if he had sold his one half share to a third party. If and when the wife actually sold the house at a later date, her capital gains liability was correspondingly reduced. A narrow exception occurred when all the property was split equally.

Transfers of real estate made on or after July 19, 1984, are now considered **tax free events.** A husband who transfers his interest in jointly owned real estate to his wife pays no capital gains tax. If and when the wife later sells the property, she pays capital gains tax on it in the same amount as if she alone had owned it all along.

A recent revision in the tax code allows each spouse a $250,000 exemption from capital gains tax on real estate which has been used as a primary residence for 2 of the past 5 years. And this exemption can be utilized every 2 years on future sales of primary residences.

Filing Status

You may file a joint return with your husband, and thereby realize maximum tax savings, as along as you have not received a final judgment of divorce separate support, or annulment by the end of the tax year. If you do file a **joint return** with your husband, you will be jointly liable with him for the entire tax, even though all or most of the income was earned by him.

If you or your husband refuse to file a joint tax return, you may have to file a return as a **married person filing separately.** However, you and your husband will have to use the same method of determining your deductions (either standard or itemized deductions) unless there is a court order of support. The rates are higher, but you will only be liable for tax on your own income.

Once your judgment of divorce has become final, you may file as a **single person.** The judgment must be final by the last day of the tax year.

You may qualify for special **head of household** filing status and be taxed at a lower rate if you have maintained the principal home for your child for more than half the year, and you have paid more than one half the cost of the household. You may file as **head of household** only if you are not married at the end of the tax year, or are considered unmarried for tax purposes because you lived apart from your husband for the last 6 months of the tax year.

Children as Dependents

As of January 1, 1985, the dependency exemption goes to the parent who has physical custody of the child, unless both parties agree otherwise. You have physical custody if the provisions of a signed separation agreement or court order state that you do, or if you made the principal home for your child for more than half the tax year.

In addition, you must be living apart from your husband with a separation agreement or court order made before the end of the tax year, or else you must have lived apart from your husband for at least the last 6 months of the tax year. Over half of your child's total support must come from you and your former spouse. Support includes money spent on food, clothing, shelter, medical and dental insurance and uninsured expenses, education, recreation, summer camp, lessons, babysitting, and other expenses of your child.

Although you may be entitled to claim your child as a dependent, you may waive the exemption for one or more years by signing IRS form 8332 which will entitle your husband to claim the exemption.

If a separation agreement or final judgment of divorce made prior to 1985 gives the exemption to the non-custodial parent, he or she must provide at least $600 per year for the support of the child. If not, the exemption goes to the parent who has provided the larger amount of support.

Chapter 14   GIVE ME SHELTER

As we all know by now, some more painfully than others, there have been numerous and devastating changes in the laws concerning the welfare of the neediest among us. "Two years and you're out" is the essence of this new deal. When I first wrote this book in 1974, we were still building public housing and waging a War on Poverty.

Unfortunately our national priorities have changed. The very idea of giving shelter, or otherwise sharing the nation's wealth, has gone out of style. Instead, we warehouse people (overnight only) in dangerously cramped and disease-infested "homeless shelters" or just let them live on the streets.

We gave up on the War on Poverty and instead took up the ill-conceived War on Drugs. Now the only public housing we are building is prisons for victimless "criminals". Casting stones and incarcerating people have become such national obsessions that to indulge them we have been willing to scrap much of the Bill of Rights, along with the great social programs of President Franklin Delano Roosevelt's New Deal.

When F.D.R. took office in 1932, one of his first acts as president was to put an end to the madness known as Prohibition. Then he set about taking care of the real needs of the American people. My hope is that we shall see his brand of enlightened leadership again soon.

If your income falls within the guidelines for a family of your size, you are entitled to a range of benefits administered by the state. You will need to apply in person at your local welfare office, which is listed in your phone book under "Massachusetts, Commonwealth of" and the subheading "Department of Transitional Assistance." The main number in Boston is (617) 348-8500, also 1-800-445-6604. If you are pregnant or you have minor children, you will receive **Aid to Families with Dependent Children.** You may be required to participate in the **Employment and Training Program.** You may qualify for **Emergency Assistance, Medical Disability Assistance or Old Age Assistance.**

The Department of Revenue will locate your husband and require him to contribute to your support. They will arrange for his wages, his pension, his property and/or his income tax refunds to be attached and applied to his support obligation. If your husband is paying support, but the amount is insufficient, you may be eligible for supplementary benefits. Your husband will make payments directly to the D.O.R. Even if he misses a payment, you will receive the full amount to which you are entitled. If you run into problems with the Department of Transitional Assistance, contact one of the **legal aid** offices listed in the Appendix. You will be able to get free legal advice on your rights. If you appeal a decision of the department, a legal aid lawyer may represent you.

If you are receiving any of the benefits described above, you will also be entitled to **food stamps** and **Medicaid.** Even if you are not eligible for financial assistance, you may qualify for food stamps and Medicaid. In addition to the above, many communities now have food pantries where you can pick up bundles of food. You may also have a community kitchen in your area where you and your children can have a free meal. Emergency shelters are available in most cities. Call hotline numbers listed below.

Housing and Homeless Shelters

If you need immediate housing assistance, you may be put off by the red tape, delay and intrusion government agencies insist on first. A call to one of the following groups should find you shelter without the hassle.

Boston Affordable Housing Coalition	(617) 267-2949
Citizens Housing and Planning Association	(617) 742-0820
Coalition for Basic Human Needs	(617) 497-0126
Massachusetts Coalition of Battered Women Services	(617) 248-0922
Massachusetts Affordable Housing Alliance, Dorchester	(617) 265-8995
Massachusetts Coalition of the Homeless	(617) 737-3508
Massachusetts Tenants Organization	(617) 367-6260

Battered Women's Center Hotlines

For legal assistance, you can call The Women's Bar Association Family Law Project for Battered Women at (617) 695-1360.

If you are in need of a safe place to hide with your children from an abusive partner, call one of the following hotline numbers.

Boston	Casa Myrna Vasquez	1-800 992-2600
	Elizabeth Stone House	(617) 522-3417
	Finex House, Inc.	(617) 288-1054
	Renewal House	(617) 566-6881
Cambridge	Transition House	(617) 661-7203
Chelsea	Harbor Me	(617) 889-2111
Fitchburg	Women's Resource Center	(978) 342-9355
Greenfield	N.E. Learning Center for Women in Transition	(413) 772-0871
Haverhill	Women's Resource Center	(978) 373-4041
Holyoke	Womanshelter/Companeras	(413) 536-1628
Hyannis	Independence House	1-800 439-6507
Lawrence	Women's Resource Center	(978) 685-2480
Lowell	Alternative House	(978) 454-1436
Malden	Services Against Family Violence	(617) 324-2221
Nantucket	Safe Place, Inc.	(508) 228-2111
New Bedford	Domestic Violence Hotline	(508) 999-6636
Newburyport	Women's Crisis Center	(978) 465-2155
Northampton	Necessities/Necesidades	(413) 586-5066
Norwood	New Hope Hotline	1-800-323-4673
Pittsfield	Women's Service Center Hotline	(413) 443-0089
Plymouth	South Shore Women's Center	(508) 746-2664
Quincy	Dove	(617) 471-1234
Salem	Help for Abused Women and Their Children	(978) 744-6841
Somerville	Respond	(617) 623-5900
Taunton	New Hope	(508) 824-5205
Waltham	Waltham Battered Women's Support Committee	1-800-899-4000
Westfield	New Beginnings	(413) 562-1920
Worcester	Abby's House	(508) 756-5486
	Daybreak	(508) 755-9030

NATIONAL Domestic Violence Hotline   1-800-799-7233   or   1-800-799-SAFE
National Hotline for Hearing Impaired Victims   1-800-787-3224

PROBATE AND FAMILY COURTS

Barnstable County Probate and Family Court   (508) 362-2511
Main Street, P. O. Box 346 Barnstable MA 02630

Berkshire County Probate and Family Court   (413) 442-6941
44 Bank Row, Pittsfield MA 01201

Bristol County Probate and Family Court   (508) 824-4004
11 Court Street, Taunton MA 02780

Dukes County Probate and Family Court   (508) 627-4703
Main Street, P. O. Box 5031, Edgartown MA 02539

Essex County Probate and Family Court   (508) 741-0201
36 Federal Street, Salem MA 01970
   additional session at
Lawrence Superior Court, 41 Appleton Street

Franklin County Probate and Family Court   (413) 774-7011
425 Main Street, Greenfield MA 01301

Hampden County Probate and Family Court   (413) 781-8100
50 State Street, Springfield MA 01103

Hampshire County Probate and Family Court   (413) 586-8500
33 King Street, Northampton MA 01060

Middlesex County Probate and Family Court   (617) 494-4533
208 Cambridge Streets, Cambridge MA 02141
   additional sessions at
Concord and Marlborough District Courts

Nantucket County Probate and Family Court   (508) 228-2669
16 Broad Street, P. O. Box 1116, Nantucket MA 02554

Norfolk County Probate and Family Court   (617) 326-7200
649 High Street, Dedham MA 02026
   additional session at
Wrentham District Court, 60 East Street

Plymouth County Probate and Family Court   (508) 747-6204
North Russell Street, P. O. Box 3640, Plymouth MA 02361
   additional session at
Brockton Superior Court, 72 Belmont Street

Suffolk County Probate and Family Court   (617) 725-8300
Old Courthouse, Pemberton Square, Boston MA 02108

Worcester County Probate and Family Court   (508) 770-0825
2 Main Street, Worcester MA 01608

DISTRICT COURTS

BARNSTABLE COUNTY

Barnstable District Court, Court House, Barnstable 02630   (508) 362-2511
also serving the towns of Yarmouth, Sandwich
Falmouth District Court, 161 Jones Road, Falmouth 02540   (508) 495-1500
also serving the towns of Bourne, Falmouth, Mashpee
Orleans District Court, 237 Rock Harbor Road, Orleans 02643   (508) 255-4700
Brewster, Chatham, Dennis, Eastham, Harwich, Provincetown, Truro, Wellfleet

BERKSHIRE COUNTY

North Adams District Court, 10 Main Street, North Adams 01247   (413) 663-5339
Branch Address - 65 Park Street, Adams 01220   (413) 743-0021
Adams, Williamstown, Clarksburg, Florida, New Ashford, Cheshire, Savoy,
Hancock, Windsor
Pittsfield District Court, 24 Wendell Avenue, Pittsfield 01201
(413) 499-0553 Hancock, Lanesborough, Peru, Hinsdale, Dalton, Washington,
Richmond, Lenox, Becket, Windsor
Great Barrington District Court, 9 Gilmore Avenue, Great Barrington 02130   (413)
528-3520   Alford, Becket, Egremont, Lee, Lenox, Monterey, Mount Washington, Otis,
New Marlborough, Sandisfield, Sheffield, Stockbridge, Tyringham, West Stockbridge

BRISTOL COUNTY

Attleboro District Court, 88 North Main Street, Attleboro 02703
(508) 222-5955 North Attleboro, Mansfield, Norton
Fall River District Court, 45 Rock Street, Fall River 02720
(508) 679-8161   Freetown, Somerset, Swansea, Westport
New Bedford District Court, 75 North Sixth Street, New Bedford 02740
(508) 999-9700   Acushnet, Dartmouth, Fairhaven, Freetown, Westport
Taunton District Court, 15 Court Street, Taunton 02780   (508) 824-4033
Berkley, Dighton, Easton, Raynham, Rehoboth, Seekonk

DUKES COUNTY

Edgartown District Court, Main Street, Edgartown 02539   (508) 627-3751
All towns on Martha's Vineyard and the Elizabeth Islands

ESSEX COUNTY

Gloucester District Court, 197 Main Street, Gloucester 01930
(978) 283-2620   Essex, Rockport
Haverhill District Court, Ginty Boulevard, P. O. Box 1389, Haverhill 01831
(978) 373-4151   Groveland, Georgetown, Boxford, West Newbury
Ipswich District Court, South Main Street, P. O. Box 246, Ipswich 01938
(978) 356-2681   Hamilton, Topsfield, Wenham
Lawrence District Court, 381 Common Street, Lawrence 01840   (978) 687-7184
Andover, Methuen, North Andover
Lynn District Court, 580 Essex Street, Lynn 01901   (6781) 598-5200
Marblehead, Nahant, Saugus, Swampscott

61

Newburyport District Court, 188 State Street, Route 1 Traffic Circle, Newburyport 01950 (978) 462-2652 Amesbury, Merrimac, Newbury, Rowley, West Newbury, Salisbury
Peabody District Court, 1 Lowell Street, P. O. Box 666 Peabody 01960 (978) 532-3100 Lynnfield
Salem District Court, 65 Washington Street, Salem 01970 (978) 744-1167 Beverly, Danvers, Middleton, Manchester

FRANKLIN COUNTY

Greenfield District Court, 425 Main Street, Greenfield 01301 (413) 774-5533 Ashfield, Bernardston, Buckland, Charlemont, Colrain, Conway, Deerfield, Gill, Hawley, Heath, Leverett, Leyden, Monroe, Montague, Northfield, Rowe, Shelburne, Shutesbury, Sunderland, Whately
Orange District Court, 1 Court Square, Orange 01364 (978) 544-8277 Athol, Erving, New Salem, Warwick, Wendell

HAMPDEN COUNTY

Chicopee District Court, 30 Church Street, Chicopee 01020 (413) 598-0099
Holyoke District Court, Court House Square, Holyoke 01040 (413) 538-9710
Palmer District Court, 234 Sykes Street, Palmer 01069 (413) 283-8916 Brimfield, Hampden, Monson, Holland, Wales, Wilbraham, Ludlow
Springfield District Court, 50 State Street, P. O. Box 2421, Springfield 01103 (413) 748-8600 Agawam, East Longmeadow, Longmeadow, West Springfield
Westfield District Court, 27 Washington Street, Westfield 01085 (413) 568-8946 Blandford, Chester, Granville, Montgomery, Russell, Southwick, Tolland

HAMPSHIRE COUNTY

Northampton District Court, 15 Gothic Street, Northampton 01060 (413) 584-7400 Amherst, Chesterfield, Cummington, Easthampton, Goshen, Hadley, Hatfield, Huntington, Middlefield, Pelham, Plainfield, Southampton, South Hadley, Westhampton, Williamsburg, Worthington
Ware District Court, 71 South Street, P. O. Box 300, Ware 01082 (413) 967-3301 Belchertown, Granby

MIDDLESEX COUNTY

Ayer District Court, 25 East Main Street, Ayer 01432 (978) 772-2100 Ashby, Boxborough, Dunstable, Groton, Littleton, Pepperell, Shirley, Townsend, Westford
Cambridge District Court, 40 Thorndike Street, P. O. Box 338, East Cambridge 02141 (617) 494-4310 Arlington Belmont
Concord District Court, 305 Walden Street, Concord 01742 (978) 369-0500 Acton, Bedford, Carlisle, Lexington, Lincoln, Maynard, Stow
Framingham District Court, 600 Concord Street, P. O. Box 828, Framingham 01701 (508) 875-7461 Ashland, Holliston, Hopkinton, Sudbury, Wayland
Lowell District Court, 41 Hurd Street, Lowell 01852 (978) 459-4101 Billerica, Chelmsford, Dracut, Tewksbury, Tyngsborough

Malden District Court, 89 Summer Street, Malden 02148 (781) 322-7500
Melrose, Everett, Wakefield
Marlborough District Court, 45 Williams Street, Marlborough 01752
(508) 485-3700 Hudson
Natick District Court, 117 East Central Street, Natick 01760
(508) 653-4332 Sherborn
Newton District Court, 1309 Washington Street, West Newton 02165
(617) 244-3600
Somerville District Court, 175 Fellsway, Somerville 02145 (617) 666-8000
Medford
Waltham District Court, 38 Linden Street, Waltham 02154 (781) 894-4500
Watertown, Weston
Woburn District Court, 30 Pleasant Street, Woburn 01801 (781) 935-4000
Burlington, North Reading, Reading, Stoneham, Wilmington, Winchester

NANTUCKET COUNTY

Nantucket District Court, 16 Broad Street, P. O. Box 1800, Nantucket 02554
(508) 228-0460

NORFOLK COUNTY

Brookline District Court, 360 Washington Street, Brookline 02146
(617) 232-4660
Dedham District Court, 631 High Street, Dedham 02026 (781) 329-4777
Dover, Needham, Norwood, Medfield, Wellesley, Westwood
Milford District Court,161 West Street, P. O. Box 370, Milford 01757
(508)473-1260 Bellingham, Hopedale, Mendon, Upton
Quincy District Court, One Dennis Ryan Parkway, Quincy 02169
(617) 471-1650 Braintree, Cohasset, Holbrook, Milton, Randolph, Weymouth
Stoughton District Court, 1288 Central Street, Stoughton 02072
(781) 344-2131 Avon, Canton, Sharon
Wrentham District Court, 60 East Street, P. O. Box 1006, Wrentham 02093
(508) 384-3106 Foxboro, Franklin, Medway, Millis, Norfolk, Plainville,
Walpole

PLYMOUTH COUNTY

Brockton District Court, 155 West Elm Street, Brockton 02401 (508) 587-8000
Abington, Bridgewater, East Bridgewater, West Bridgewater, Whitman
Hingham District Court, 28 George Washington Boulevard, Hingham 02043
(781) 749-7000 Hanover, Hull, Norwell, Rockland, Scituate
Plymouth District Court, Russell Street, Plymouth 02360 (508) 747-0500
Duxbury, Halifax, Hanson, Kingston, Marshfield, Pembroke, Plympton
Wareham District Court, 2200 Cranberry Highway, West Wareham 02576
(508) 295-8300 Carver, Lakeville, Marion, Mattapoisett, Middleboro,
Rochester

SUFFOLK COUNTY

Brighton District Court, 52 Academy Hill Road, Brighton 02135
(617) 782-6521
Charlestown District Court, 3 City Square, Charlestown 02129
(617) 242-5400
Chelsea District Court, Temporary Address: 121 Third Street, East
Cambridge 02141 (617) 252-0763 Revere
Dorchester District Court, Court Annex, 450 Washington Street, Dorchester
02124 (617) 288-9500
East Boston District Court, 37 Meridian Street, East Boston 02128
(617) 569-7550 Winthrop
Roxbury District Court, 85 Warren Street, Roxbury 02119 (617) 427-7000
South Boston District Court, 535 East Broadway, South Boston 02127
(617) 268-9292
West Roxbury District Court, 445 Arborway, Forest Hills, Mailing
Address is Jamaica Plain 02130 (617) 522-4710

WORCESTER COUNTY

Clinton District Court, Routes 62 and 70, P. O. Box 30, Clinton 01510
(978) 368-7811 Berlin, Bolton, Boylston, Harvard, Lancaster, Sterling
Dudley District Court, West Main Street, P.O. Box 100, Dudley 01571
(508) 943-7123 Charlton, Oxford, Southbridge, Sturbridge, Webster
East Brookfield District Court, 544 East Main Street, East Brookfield 01515
(508) 885-6305,06 Brookfield, East Brookfield, North Brookfield, West
Brookfield, Leicester, Spencer, Warren, Hardwick, New Braintree
Fitchburg District Court, 100 Elm Street, Fitchburg 01420 (978) 345-2111
Ashburnham, Lunenburg
Gardner District Court, 108 Matthews Street, P. O. Box 40, Gardner 01440
(978) 632-2373,4,5 Hubbardston, Petersham, Phillipston, Royalston, Templeton,
Westminster
Leominster District Court, 25 School Street, Leominster 01453 (978) 537-3722
Princeton
Milford District Court, 161 West Street, P. O. Box 370, Milford 01757
(508) 473-1260 Mendon, Upton, Hopedale, Bellingham
Orange District Court, 1 Court Square, Orange 01364 (978) 544-8277 Athol,
Erving, New Salem, Warwick, Wendell
Uxbridge District Court, South Main Street, P. O. Box 580, Uxbridge 01569
(508) 278-2454 Blackstone, Douglas, Millville, Northbridge, Sutton
Westborough District Court, 175 Milk Street, Westborough 01581 (508) 366-8266
Grafton, Northborough, Shrewsbury, Southborough
Winchendon District Court, 80 Central Street, P. O. Box 309, Winchendon 01475
(978) 297-0156
Worcester District Court, 50 Harvard Street, Worcester 01608 (508) 757-8350
Auburn, Barre, Holden, Millbury, Oakham, Paxton, Rutland, West Boylston

Each district court serves the town it is located in,
and also the other towns listed.

LEGAL AID OFFICES

STATEWIDE

Massachusetts Bar Association Community Services Program,
20 West Street, Boston 02111 (617) 338-0570

BOSTON AREA

Boston Bar Association Volunteer Lawyers Project, 29 Temple Place, Boston
02111 (617) 423-0648 Boston and parts of Suffolk and Middlesex Counties

Boston College Legal Assistance Bureau, 24 Crescent Street, Waltham 02154
(781) 893-4793 Newton, Waltham, Watertown

Cambridge & Somerville Legal Services, 432 Columbia Street, Cambridge 02141
(617) 494-1800 also Arlington, Belmont, Winchester, Woburn

Community Legal Services & Counseling Center, One West Street, Cambridge 02139
(617) 661-1010 Arlington, Belmont, Boston, Brookline, Cambridge, Chelsea,
Everett, Medford, Somerville, Watertown

Greater Boston Legal Services, 197 Friend Street, Boston 02114
(617) 371-1234

Harvard Legal Aid Bureau, 1511 Massachusetts Avenue, Cambridge 02138
(617) 495-4408 Middlesex and Suffolk Counties

Jamaica Plain Legal Services, 122 Boylston Street, Jamaica Plain 02130
(617) 522-3003

New England School of Law Legal Services, 46 Church Street, Boston 02116
(617) 422-7380 Boston, Everett, Malden, Wakefield

Suffolk Legal Services, 278 Broadway, Chelsea 02150
(617) 884-7568 Chelsea and Revere

CAPE COD

Legal Services for Cape Cod & Islands, 460 West Main Street, Hyannis 02601
(508) 775-7020 Barnstable, Dukes and Nantucket Counties
  18 Main Street Ext., Plymouth 02360 (508) 746-2777 Eastern Plymouth County

FRAMINGHAM AREA

South Middlesex Legal Services, Inc., 300 Howard Street, Framingham 01702
(508) 620-1830 Southern and Central Middlesex and Western Norfolk Counties

continued next page

LEGAL AID OFFICES, continued

<u>NORTHEASTERN MASSACHUSETTS</u>

Merrimack Valley Legal Services, Inc., 11 Lawrence Street, Suite 324, Lawrence 01840, (978) 687-1177, and 35 John Street, Suite 302, Lowell 01852 (978) 458-1465 Northern Middlesex County and Essex County

Neighborhood Legal Services, 37 Friend Street, Lynn 01902 (781) 599-7730 11 Lawrence Street, Suite 300, Lawrence 01840 (978) 686-6900 Northern Middlesex County and Essex County

<u>SOUTHEASTERN MASSACHUSETTS</u>

Southeastern Massachusetts Legal Assistance Corp., 231 Main Street, Suite 201, Brockton 02401 (508) 586-2110 1-800-244-8393 Norfolk and Plymouth Counties

Southeastern Massachusetts Legal Assistance Corp., 558 Pleasant Street, Suite 201, New Bedford 02740 (508) 997-9781
   Attleboro – 7 North Main Street, Suite 221 (508) 226-6416
   Fall River – 30 Third Street, 3rd Floor (508) 676-6265 1-800-287-3777
   New Bedford – 21 South Sixth Street (508) 979-7150 1-800-929-9721
   Taunton – 71 Main Street, Suite 2400 (508) 880-6704
          Hispanic Outreach (508) 822-3207

<u>CENTRAL MASSACHUSETTS</u>

Legal Assistance Corporation of Central Massachusetts, 405 Main Street, 4th Floor, Worcester 01608 (508) 752-3718, serves all cities and towns in Worcester County
   717 Main Street, Suite 9, Fitchburg 01420 (978) 345-0301

<u>WESTERN MASSACHUSETTS</u>

Western Massachusetts Legal Services
   Greenfield Office, 55 Federal Street, Greenfield 01301 (413) 774-3747 Franklin and Hampshire Counties

   Holyoke Office, 57 Suffolk Street, 4th Floor, Holyoke 01040 (413) 536-2420 Berkshire, Franklin and Hampshire Counties

   Northampton Office, 20 Hampton Avenue, Suite 100, Northampton 01060 (413) 584-4034 all of Franklin County

   Pittsfield Office, 152 North Street, Suite 155, Pittsfield 01201 (413) 499-1950 Berkshire County

   Springfield Office, 145 State Street, Springfield 01103 (413) 781-7814 Northern Hampden County

Children; care and custody; modification of orders; provisions for
education and health insurance; pre-existing orders for maintenance

Upon a judgment for divorce, the court may make such judgment as it
considers expedient relative to the care, custody and maintenance of the
minor children of the parties and may determine with which of the parents
the children or any of them shall remain or may award their custody to
some third person if it seems expedient or for the benefit of the children.

Upon a complaint after a divorce, filed by either parent or by a next
friend on behalf of the children after notice to both parents, the court may
make a judgment modifying its earlier judgment as to the care and custody of
the minor children of the parties provided that the court finds that a material and substantial change in the circumstances of the parties has occurred
and the judgment of modification is necessary in the best interests of the
children.

In furtherance of the public policy that dependent children shall be
maintained as completely as possible from the resources of their parents and
upon a complaint filed after a judgment of divorce, orders of maintenance
and for support of minor children shall be modified if there is an inconsistency between the amount of the existing order and the amount that would
result from application of the child support guidelines promulgated by the
chief justice for administration and management or if there is a need to
provide for the health care coverage of the child.

A modification to provide for the health care coverage of the child
shall be entered whether or not a modification in the amount of child
support is necessary.

There shall be a rebuttable presumption that the amount of the order
which would result from the application of the guidelines is the appropriate
amount of child support to be ordered. If, after taking into consideration
the best interests of the child, the court determines that a party has
overcome such presumption, the court shall make specific written findings
indicating the amount of the order that would result from application of
the guidelines; that the guidelines amount would be unjust or inappropriate
under the circumstances; the specific facts of the case which justify
departure from the guidelines; and that such departure is consistent with
the best interests of the child. The order shall be modified accordingly
unless the inconsistency between the amount of the existing order and the
amount of the order that would result from application of the guidelines
is due to the fact that the amount of the existing order resulted from a
rebuttal of the guidelines and that there has been no change in the circumstances which resulted in such rebuttal; provided, however, that even if the
specific facts that justified departure from the guidelines upon entry of
the existing order remain in effect, the order shall be modified in accordance with the guidelines unless the court finds that the guidelines amount
would be unjust or inappropriate under the circumstances and that the
existing order is consistent with the best interests of the child.

A modification of child support may enter notwithstanding an agreement of the parents that has independent legal significance.

The court may make appropriate orders of maintenance, support and education of any child who has attained age eighteen but who has not attained age twenty-one and who is domiciled in the home of a parent, and is principally dependent upon said parent for maintenance. The court may make appropriate orders of maintenance, support and education for any child who has attained age twenty-one but who has not attained age twenty-three, if such child is domiciled in the home of a parent, and is principally dependent upon said parent for maintenance due to the enrollment of such child in an educational program, excluding educational costs beyond an undergraduate degree.

When the court makes an order for maintenance or support of a child, said court shall determine whether the obligor under such order has health insurance or other health coverage on a group plan available to him through an employer or organization or has health insurance or other health coverage available to him at a reasonable cost that may be extended to cover the child for whom support is ordered. When said court has determined that the obligor has such insurance or coverage available to him, said court shall include in the support order a requirement that the obligor exercise the option of additional coverage in favor of the child or obtain coverage for the child.

When a court makes an order for maintenance or support, the court shall determine whether the obligor under such order is responsible for the maintenance or support of any other children of the obligor, even if a court order for such maintenance or support does not exist, or whether the obligor under such order is under a preexisting order for the maintenance or support of any other children from a previous marriage, or whether the obligor under such order is under a preexisting order for the maintenance or support of any other children born out of wedlock. If the court determines that such responsibility does, in fact, exist and that such obligor is fulfilling such responsibility such court shall take into consideration such responsibility in setting the amount to be paid under the current order for maintenance or support.

No court shall make an order providing visitation rights to a parent who has been convicted of murder in the first degree of the other parent of the child who is the subject of the order, unless such child is of suitable age to signify his assent and assents to such order; provided, further, that until such order is issued, no person shall visit, with the child present, a parent who has been convicted of murder in the first degree of the other parent of the child without the consent of the child's custodian or legal guardian.

MASSACHUSETTS GENERAL LAWS, CHAPTER 208, SECTION 31

Custody

For the purposes of this section, the following words shall have the following meaning unless the context requires otherwise:

"Sole legal custody", one parent shall have the right and responsibility to make major decisions regarding the child's welfare including matters of education, medical care and emotional, moral and religious development.

"Shared legal custody", continued mutual responsibility and involvement by both parents in major decisions regarding the child's welfare including matters of education, medical care and emotional, moral and religious development.

"Sole physical custody", a child shall reside with and be under the supervision of one parent, subject to reasonable visitation by the other parent, unless the court determines that such visitation would not be in the best interest of the child.

"Shared physical custody", a child shall have periods of residing with and being under the supervision of each parent; provided, however, that physical custody shall be shared by the parents in such a way as to assure a child frequent and continued contact with both parents.

In making an order or judgment relative to the custody of children, the rights of the parents shall in the absence of misconduct, be held to be equal, and the happiness and welfare of the children shall determine their custody. When considering the happiness and welfare of the child, the court shall consider whether or not the child's present or past living conditions adversely affect his physical, mental, moral or emotional health.

Upon the filing of an action in accordance with the provisions of this section, section twenty-eight of this chapter, or section thirty-two of chapter two hundred and nine and until a judgment on the merits is rendered, absent emergency conditions, abuse or neglect, the parents shall have temporary shared legal custody of any minor child of the marriage; provided, however, that the judge may enter an order for temporary sole legal custody for one parent if written findings are made that such shared custody would not be in the best interest of the child. Nothing herein shall be construed to create any presumption of temporary shared physical custody.

In determining whether temporary shared legal custody would not be in the best interest of the child, the court shall consider all relevant facts including, but not limited to, whether any member of the family has been the perpetrator of domestic violence, abuses alcohol or other drugs or has deserted the child and whether the parties have a history of being able and willing to cooperate in matters concerning the child.

If, despite the prior or current issuance of a restraining order against one parent pursuant to chapter two hundred and nine A, the court orders shared legal or physical custody either as a temporary order or at a trial on the merits, the court shall provide written findings to support such shared custody order.

There shall be no presumption either in favor of or against shared legal or physical custody at the time of the trial on the merits.

At the trial on the merits, if the issue of custody is contested and either party seeks shared legal or physical custody, the parties, jointly or individually, shall submit to the court at the trial a shared custody implementation plan setting forth the details of shared custody including, but not limited to, the child's education; the child's health care; procedures for resolving disputes between the parties with respect to child-raising decisions and duties; and the periods of time during which each party will have the child reside or visit with him, including holidays and vacations, or the procedure by which such periods of time shall be determined.

At the trial on the merits, the court shall consider the shared custody implementation plans submitted by the parties. The court may issue a shared legal and physical custody order and, in conjunction therewith, may accept the shared custody implementation plan submitted by either party or by the parties jointly or may issue a plan modifying the plan or plans submitted by the parties. The court may also reject the plan and issue a sole legal and physical custody award to either parent. A shared custody implementation plan issued or accepted by the court shall become part of the judgment in the action, together with any other appropriate custody orders and orders regarding the responsibility of the parties for the support of the child.

Provisions regarding shared custody contained in an agreement executed by the parties and submitted to the court for its approval that addresses the details of shared custody shall be deemed to constitute a shared custody implementation plan for purposes of this section.

An award of shared legal or physical custody shall not affect a parent's responsibility for child support. An order of shared custody shall not constitute grounds for modifying a support order absent demonstrated economic impact that is an otherwise sufficient basis warranting modification.

The entry of an order or judgment relative to the custody of minor children shall not negate or impede the ability of the non-custodial parent to have access to the academic, medical, hospital or other health records of the child, as he would have had if the custody order or judgment had not been entered; provided, however, that if a court has issued an order to vacate against the non-custodial parent or an order prohibiting the non-custodial parent from imposing any restraint upon the personal liberty of the other parent or if nondisclosure of the present or prior address of the child or a party is necessary to ensure the health, safety or welfare of such child or party, the court may order that any part of such record pertaining to such address shall not be disclosed to such non-custodial parent.

Where the parents have reached an agreement providing for the custody of the children, the court may enter an order in accordance with such agreement, unless specific findings are made by the court indicating that such an order would not be in the best interests of the children.

MASSACHUSETTS GENERAL LAWS, CHAPTER 208, SECTION 34

Alimony and Property

Upon divorce or upon a complaint in an action brought at any time after a divorce, whether such a divorce has been adjudged in this commonwealth or another jurisdiction, the court of the commonwealth, provided there is personal jurisdiction over both parties, may make a judgment for either of the parties to pay alimony to the other.

In addition to or in lieu of a judgment to pay alimony, the court may assign to either husband or wife all or any part of the estate of the other, including but not limited to, all vested and nonvested benefits, rights and funds accrued during the marriage and which shall include, but not be limited to, retirement benefits, military retirement benefits if qualified under and to the extent provided by federal law, pension, profit-sharing, annuity, deferred compensation and insurance.

In determining the amount of alimony, if any, to be paid, or in fixing the nature and value of the property, if any, to be so assigned, the court, after hearing the witnesses, if any, of each party, shall consider the length of the marriage, the conduct of the parties during the marriage, the age, health, station, occupation, amount and sources of income, vocational skills, employability, estate, liabilities and needs of each of the parties and the opportunity of each for future acquisition of capital assets and income.

In fixing the nature and value of the property to be so assigned, the court shall also consider the present and future needs of the dependent children of the marriage.

The court may also consider the contribution of each of the parties in the acquisition, preservation or appreciation in value of their respective estates and the contribution of each of the parties as a homemaker to the family unit.

When the court makes an order for alimony on behalf of a spouse, said court shall determine whether the obligor under such order has health insurance or other health coverage available to him through an employer or organization or has health insurance or other health coverage available to him at reasonable cost that may be extended to cover the spouse for whom support is ordered.

When said court has determined that the obligor has such insurance or coverage available to him, said court shall include in the support order a requirement that the obligor do one of the following: exercise the option of additional coverage in favor of the spouse, obtain coverage for the spouse, or reimburse the spouse for the cost of health insurance.

In no event shall the order for alimony be reduced as a result of the obligor's cost for health insurance coverage for the spouse.

CHILD SUPPORT GUIDELINES

N.B. THESE GUIDELINES APPLY TO CURRENT CHILD SUPPORT ONLY. THEY DO NOT APPLY TO ALIMONY, THE DIVISION OF MARITAL PROPERTY, THE PAYMENT OF ARREARS, RESTITUTION, OR REIMBURSEMENT, NOR DO THEY APPLY WHERE THE PARTIES HAVE MADE AN AGREEMENT WHICH IS APPROVED BY THE COURT AND IS FOUND BY THE COURT TO BE FAIR AND REASONABLE, AND MAKES ADEQUATE PROVISION FOR THE SUPPORT OF THE CHILD.

THERE SHALL BE A PRESUMPTION THAT THESE GUIDELINES APPLY, ABSENT AGREEMENT OF THE PARTIES, IN ALL CASES SEEKING THE ESTABLISHMENT OR MODIFICATION OF A CHILD SUPPORT ORDER. A SPECIFIC, WRITTEN FINDING THAT THE GUIDELINES WOULD BE UNJUST OR INAPPROPRIATE AND THAT THE BEST INTERESTS OF THE CHILD HAVE BEEN CONSIDERED IN A PARTICULAR CASE SHALL BE SUFFICIENT TO REBUT THE PRESUMPTION IN THAT CASE.

The child support guidelines are formulated to be used by the justices of the Trial Court, whether the parents of the children are married or unmarried, in setting temporary, permanent or final orders for current child support, in deciding whether to approve agreements for child support, and in deciding cases that are before the court to modify existing orders. A modification may be allowed upon showing of a discrepancy of 20% or more between an established order and a proposed new order calculated under these guidelines. The presumption establishing a proposed new order may be rebutted in cases where the amount of support required under the guidelines is due to the fact that the amount of the current support order resulted from a rebuttal of the guideline amount or by an allowance of an agreement of the parties and there has not been a change in the circumstances which resulted in a rebuttal of the guideline amount. The guidelines are intended to be of assistance to members of the bar and to litigants in determining what level of payment would be expected of them given the relative income levels of the parties.

In establishing the guidelines, due consideration has been given to the following principles:

1) To minimize the economic impact on the child of family breakup;
2) To encourage joint parental responsibility for child support in proportion to, or as a percentage of income;
3) To provide the standards of living the child would have enjoyed had the family been intact;
4) To meet the child's survival needs in the first instance, but to the extent either parent enjoys that higher standard of living to entitle the child to enjoy that higher standard;
5) To protect a subsistence level of income of parents at the low end of the income range whether or not they are on public assistance;
6) To take into account the non-monetary contributions of both the custodial and non-custodial parents;
7) To minimize problems of proof for the parties and of administration for the courts;
8) To allow for orders and wage assignments that can be adjusted as income increases or decreases.

I.INCOME DEFINITION

A. For purposes of these guidelines, income is defined as gross income from whatever source. Those sources include but are not limited to the following:

1) salaries and wages (including overtime and tips) and income from self-employment (except in certain instances, see B, below)
2) commissions
3) severamce pay

4) royalties
5) bonuses
6) interest and dividends
7) income derived from businesses/partnerships
8) social security
9) veteran's benefits
10) insurance benefits (including those received for disability and personal injury
11) worker's compensation
12) unemployment compensation
13) pensions
14) annuities
15) income from trusts
16) capital gains in real and personal property transactions to the extent that they represent a regular source of income
17) spousal support received from a person not a party to the order
18) contractual agreements
19) perquisites or in kind compensation to the extent that they represent a regular source of income
20) unearned income of children (in the court's discretion)
21) income from life insurance or endowment contracts
22) income from interest in an estate (direct or through a trust)
23) lottery or gambling winnings received either in a lump sum or in the form of an annuity
24) prizes or awards
25) net rental income
26) funds received from earned income credit

B. In individual cases, the court may choose to disregard overtime income or income derived from a second job. However, consideration of such income may be appropriate in certain instances such as those where such income constituted a regular source of income when the family was intact.

II. FACTORS TO BE CONSIDERED IN SETTING THE CHILD SUPPORT ORDER

A. Relationship to Alimony or Separate Maintenance Payments

So long as the standard of living of the children is not diminished, these guidelines do not preclude the court from deciding that any order be denominated in whole or in part as alimony or a separate maintenance payment. It is the responsibility of counsel representing the parties to present the tax consequences of proposed orders to the court.

B. Claims of Personal Exemptions for Child Dependents

In setting a support order, the court may make an order regarding the claims of personal exemptions for child dependents between the parties to the extent permitted by law.

C. Minimum and Maximum Levels

The guidelines recognize the principle that, in many instances, to maintain a domicile and a reasonable standard of living for the minor children, the custodial parent will choose to work. In those cases, a disregard of gross income of the custodial parent is to be applied up to a maximum of $15,000. The formula in these guidelines is intended to be adjusted where the income of the custodial parent exceeds the $15,000 disregard after consideration of day care expenses.

These guidelines are also intended to insure a minimum subsistence level for those non-custodial parents whose income is less than $125 per week.

However, it is the obligation of all parents to contribute to the support of their children. To that end, in all cases, a minimum order of $50 ($11.55 per week) per month should enter. This minimum should not be construed as limiting the court's ability to set a higher order, should circumstances permit.

Where the court makes a determination that either or both of the parties is either purposely unemployed or underemployed, the section of this guideline entitled ATTRIBUTION OF INCOME should be consulted.

These guidelines are not meant to apply where the combined gross income of the parties exceeds $100,000 or where the gross income of the non-custodial parent exceeds $75,000. In cases where income exceeds these limits, the court should consider the award of support at the $75,000/$100,000 level as a minimum presumptive level of support to be awarded. Additional amounts of child support may be awarded at the judge's discretion.

D. Custody and Visitation

1) Custody

These guidelines are based upon traditional custody and visitation arrangements. Where the parties agree to shared physical custody or the court determines that shared physical custody is in the best interests of the children, these guidelines are not applicable. The guidelines are also not meant to apply for cases in which there is split physical custody, i.e., each parent has physical custody of one or more children.

2) Visitation

These guidelines recognize that children must be allowed to enjoy the society and companionship of both parents to the greatest extent possible. The court may adjust the amount of child support beyond the 2 percent range (see Basic Order, Section III A) after taking into consideration the parties' actual time sharing with the children and the relative resources, expenses and living standards of the two households.

In some instances, the non-custodial parent may incur extraordinary travel-related expenses in order to exercise court ordered visitation rights. To foster parental involvement with the children, the court may wish to consider such extraordinary expenses in determining the support order.

E. Childcare as Defined by Internal Revenue Code Section 21

The basic child support obligation set out in the guidelines includes the non-custodial parent's share of day care expenses. Child care expenses are not seen as a separate support item and responsibility for them resides with the custodial parent.

The reasonable cost of day care actually paid is to be subtracted from the custodial parent's gross income before the disregard formula is applied.

F. Age of the Children

To reflect the rising costs of raising children, age has been broken down into four groups: 0-6, 7-12, 13-18, and over 18. A single adjustment to the basic order should be made based on the age of the oldest child for whom support is to be ordered. The support order where the oldest child is six or under should be the basic support order according to the schedule. Where the oldest child is 7-12, the order should be increased by 10 percent of the basic order amount. Where the oldest child is between the ages of 13 and 18, the order should be increased by 15 percent of the basic order amount. For cases involving children over the age of 18, to the extent permitted by the General Laws, the amount of the order, if any will be left to the court's discretion.

Where the parties file an agreement with the court that allows for private payment between the parties, it is suggested that the incremental age issue be addressed in the agreement.

74

G. Health Insurance, Uninsured, and Extraordinary Medical Expenses
1) Health Insurance

When the court makes an order for child support, the court shall determine whether the obligor under the order has health insurance on a group plan available to him/her through an employer or organization or has health insurance or other health coverage available to him/her at reasonable cost that may be extended to cover the child for whom support is ordered. When the court makes a determination that the obligor has such coverage, the court shall include in the support order a requirement that the obligor exercise the option of additional coverage in favor of such child, unless the obligee has already provided such coverage for the child at a lesser cost (except for health insurance funded under public assistance programs), or has and prefers to continue such coverage irrespective of cost.

If family health coverage is to be provided by the obligor, the support order should be reduced by one half the cost of family coverage. It is the responsibility of the obligor under the support order who is seeking such a reduction in the order to produce proof satisfactory to the court of the existence of such family coverage under the plan, or no such reduction shall be allowed. However, there shall be no reduction if the obligor has a pre-existing family health insurance policy which could be amended to name the additional dependents to the policy at no cost to the obligor. Should health insurance not be provided for any period for which it is ordered, the credit for the premium payment shall be revoked and the order shall be increased by the amount of the credit during the period of noncompliance.

If family health coverage is to be provided by the obligee, the support order should be increased by one half the cost of the coverage. It is the responsibility of the obligee who is seeking an increase in the order to produce proof satisfactory to the court of the existence of such family coverage under the plan, or no such increase shall be allowed. However, there shall be no increase if the obligee has a pre-existing family health insurance policy which could be amended to name the additional dependents at no cost to the obligee. Should health insurance not be provided for any period for which it is ordered, the increase allowed for the premium payment shall be revoked and the order shall be decreased during the period when health insurance is not provided.

2) Routine Uninsured Medical and Dental Expenses

The custodial parent shall be responsible for the payment of the first $100 per child per year for routine medical and dental expenses. For amounts above that limit, the court shall allocate costs on a case by case basis. No reduction in the child support order should be allowed.

3) Uninsured Extraordinary Medical and Dental Expenses

The payment of uninsured extraordinary medical and dental expenses incurred by the minor children, absent agreement of the parties, shall be treated on a case by case basis. (Example: orthodontia, psychological/ psychiatric counseling, etc.) In such cases, where the court makes a determination that such medical and dental services are necessary and are in the best interests of the child, consideration toward a reduction in the child support order should be given.

H. Attribution of Income

If the court makes a determination that either or both parties is earning substantially less than he or she could through reasonable effort, the court may consider potential earning capacity rather than actual earnings. In making this determination, the court shall take into consideration the education, training, and past employment history of the party. These standards are intended to be applied where a finding has been made that the party is capable of working and is unemployed, working part-time or is working a job, trade or profession other than that for which he/she has been trained.

This determination is not intended to be applied to a custodial parent with children who are under the age of six living in the home.

I. Prior Orders for Support

To the extent that prior orders for spousal and child support are **actually** being paid, the court should deduct those payments from the gross income before applying the formula to determine the child support order. This section applies only to orders for child support for children **other than** those who are the subject of the pending action.

J. Expenses of Subsequent Families

In instances where the non-custodial parent has remarried and has children by a subsequent marriage, the court should examine such circumstances closely to determine in the allocation of available resources whether consideration beyond Part II Section I (Prior Orders of Support) should be given when the custodial parent of children born of the first marriage or subsequent marriages appears before the court seeking a modification of the existing child support order. Expenses of a subsequent family may be used as a defense to a request to modify an order seeking an increase in the existing order but, such expenses should not be considered a reason to decrease existing prior orders. In actions pursuant to G.L.c.209C, this paragraph shall be construed to apply equally to children born out of wedlock.

III CHILD SUPPORT OBLIGATION SCHEDULE

A. Basic Order

The basic child support obligation based upon the income of the non-custodial parent, is as follows:

Gross Weekly Income	Number of Children		
	1	2	3
$0 – $125	Discretion of the court, but not less than $50 per month		
$125 – $200	15%(+/-2%)	18%(+/-2%)	21%(+/-2%)
$201 – $500	25%(+/-2%)	28%(+/-2%)	31%(+/-2%)
$501 – max.	27%(+/-2%)	30%(+/-2%)	33%(+/-2%)

Within the discretion of the court, and in consideration of the totality of the circumstances of the parties, the order may be either increased or decreased by 2 percent. Where the court must set a support order where there are more than three children, the minimum order is to be no less than that contained in this guideline for three children, to be increased within the discretion of the court depending upon the circumstances of each case.

B. Age Differential

The above orders are to be increased to reflect the cost of raising older children. The following percentages are intended to be applied to the age of the oldest child in the household for whom support is sought under the pending action.

Age of Oldest Child	Percentage Increase
0 – 6	Basic Order applies
7 – 12	Basic Order + 10% of Basic Order
13 – 18	Basic Order + 15% of Basic Order
Over 18	Discretion of the court (and if statute permits)

C. Custodial Parent Income Adjustment

Where the custodial parent works and earns income in excess of $15,000 after consideration of day care expenses, the support order is to be reduced by the percentage that the excess represents in relation to the combined incomes of both parents minus the custodial parent's disregard.

76

Commonwealth of Massachusetts
The Trial Court

MIDDLESEX Division   Probate and Family Court Department   Docket No. _____

MOLLY BROWN   vs.   DESMOND BROWN

Worksheet
Child Support Guidelines

Worksheet Completed By __MOLLY BROWN__ Date Completed __5-8-98__

All provisions of the Guidelines (pp. 1-6) should be reviewed prior to the completion of the worksheet. These guidelines will apply (absent a prior agreement acceptable to both parties) in cases where combined gross income of both parties does not exceed $100,000.00 and where the income of the non-custodial parent does not exceed $75,000.00.

1. **Basic Order**
   a) Non-custodial gross weekly income (less prior support orders actually paid, for child/family other than the family seeking this order) $ __865__
   b) % of gross/number of children (from chart III A) __30__ %
   c) Basic order (a)x(b)   (A) $ __260__

2. **Adjustment For Ages of Children**
   a) Age of oldest child __10__
   b) % of increase for age (from chart III B) __10__ %
   c) Age add on (2b)x(A) $ __26__
   d) Adjusted order (A) + (2c)   (B) $ __286__

3. **Custodial Parent Income Adjustment**
   a) Custodial parent gross income $ __29,000__
   b) Less $15,000.00   −15,000.00
   c) Less day care cost (annual)   − __5,000__
   d) Custodial adjusted gross $ __9,000__
   e) Non-custodial gross (annual) $ __45,000__
   f) Total available gross 3(d) + 3(e) $ __54,000__
   g) Line 3(d) __9,000__ Line 3(f) __54,000__
   h) 3(d) divided by 3(f) __17__ per cent
   i) Adjustment for custodial income (Line 3h %) x (B)   (C) $ __49__

4. **Calculation of Final Order**
   a) Adjusted order (B) above   (B) $ __286__
   b) Less adjustment for income (C) above   (C) − __49__
   c) Less 50% of weekly cost to obligor of family group health insurance [under the provisions of section G(1)]   − __20__

   or

   Plus 50% weekly cost of obligee's family group health insurance [under the provisions of section G(1)]   + _____

   Weekly Support Order (B) − (C) ± 4(c)   77 $ __217__

CJ-D 304 (1/98)

EXPLANATION OF CHILD SUPPORT GUIDELINES SAMPLE WORKSHEET

This sample **Child Support Guidelines** worksheet was completed by Molly and Desmond Brown, our hypothetical couple, who then reached the Separation Agreement found on pages 24-29 and filed the joint petition for a no fault divorce and related documents in the Appendix.

Desmond and Molly have two children, Stephen age 10 and Michael age 4. The child care cost for Michael is $5,000 per year.

Molly earns $29,000 per year. Desmond's gross annual income (before taxes) is $45,000.

Item 1. Basic Order

Since Desmond's $865 gross weekly income is over $500, he will be paying 30% of it as support for his two children. The basic child support order is $260, which is 30% of $865.

Item 2. Adjustment for Ages of Children

Stephen, the oldest child, is 10. Therefor, Desmond will pay $26 more, an additional 10% of the basic order. The adjusted order is now $286.

Item 3. Custodial Parent Income Adjustment

Because Molly works and earns over $15,000 per year, there is a downward adjustment in the child support amount.

Molly gets a $15,000 credit against her $29,000 income for basic custodial parent expenses. She gets an additional $5,000 credit for the actual amount she is spending on day care for Michael.

Molly's adjusted gross income is now $9,000. This is divided by the total available gross income which in this case is $54,000, or Molly's $9,000 plus Desmond's $45,000, resulting in a 17% reduction in the child support amount. Thus, $49 (17% of $286) is deducted from the $286 child support amount computed in Item 2.

Item 4. Calculation of Final Order

Because Desmond pays $40 per week for medical insurance, there is another reduction in the child support in the amount of $20, for one half of his cost for the insurance. Thus, the weekly support paid by Desmond will be $217.

PLEASE NOTE, the guidelines have just been amended to provide a credit of 50% of the cost of medical insurance paid by the custodial parent (or "obligee"). For example, if Molly were paying $40 weekly for medical insurance, the child support amount paid by Desmond would be $257 per week, computed as follows: $286 less $49 plus $20.

SUPPLEMENTAL RULE 409 CASE MANAGEMENT CONFERENCE

(a) Conduct of Case Management Conference. Any party to any matter filed in the Probate and Family Court may request a case management conference 45 days after service of the complaint, with notice to the other side of said request, or the court may order a case management conference at any time. At the conference the court may:

(1) explore the possibility of settlement;

(2) identify or formulate (or order the attorneys to formulate) the principle issues and contentions; and

(3) prepare (or order the attorneys to prepare) a discovery schedule and discovery plan that, if the court deems appropriate, might:
(i) identify and limit the volume of discovery available in order to avoid unnecessary or unduly burdensome or expensive discovery;
(ii) sequence discovery into two or more stages;
(iii)set time limits for the completion of discovery;

(4) establish deadlines for filing motions and a time framework for their disposition;
(5) explore any other matter that the court determines is appropriate for the fair and efficient management of the litigation including but not limited to the use of Alternate Dispute Resolution (ADR) mechanisms.

(b) Obligation of Counsel to Confer. Prior to the case management conference the court may require counsel for the parties to confer for the purpose of preparing a joint statement containing

(1) an agenda of matters that one or more parties believe should be addressed at the conference; and

(2) a proposed schedule of deadlines and dates through trial. If no agreement is reached on said schedule, each party shall submit a proposed schedule. This statement is to be filed with the court no later than 5 business days prior to the case management conference.

(3) certifications signed by counsel and by an authorized representative of each party affirming that each party and that party's counsel have conferred with a view to establishing a budget for the costs of conducting the full course - and various alternative course - of the litigation.

(c) Additional Case Management Conferences. Nothing in this rule shall be construed to prevent the convening of additional case management conferences by the court as may be thought appropriate in the circumstances of the particular case. In any event, a conference should not be terminated without counsel being instructed as to when and for what purpose they are to return to the court.

SUPLEMENTAL RULE 410 MANDATORY SELF-DISCLOSURE

(a) Initial Disclosures.

(1) Except as otherwise agreed by the parties or odered by the court, each party shall deliver to the other within 45 days from the date of service of the summons the following documents:

(a) The parties' federal and state income tax returns and schedules for the past 3 years and any non-public, limited partnership and privately held corporate returns for any entity in which either party has an interest together with all supporting documentation for tax returns, including but not limited to W-2s, 1099s, K-1, Schedule C and Schedule E.

(b) Statements for the past 3 years for all bank accounts held in the name of either party individually or jointly, or in the name of another person for the benefit of either party, or held by either party for the benefit of the parties' minor child(ren).

(c) The 4 most recent pay stubs from each employer for whom the party worked.

(d) Documentation regarding the cost and nature of available health insurance coverage.

(e) Statements for the past 3 years for any securities, stocks, bonds, notes or obligations, certificates of deposit owned or held by either party or held by either party for the benefit of the parties' minor child(ren), 401K statements, IRA statements, and pension plan statements for all accounts listed on the 401 financial statement.

(f) Copies of any loan or mortgage applications made, prepared or submitted by either party within the last 3 years prior to the filing of the complaint for divorce.

(g) Copies of any financial statement and/or statement of assets and liabilities prepared by either party within the last 3 years prior to the filing of the complaint for divorce.

(2) The parties shall supplement all disclosures as material changes occur during the progress of the case. Neither party shall be permitted to file any discovery motions prior to making the initial disclosure as described herein.

(b) Unavailability of Documents

In the event that either party does not have any of the documents required pursuant to this Rule or has not been able to obtain them in a timely fashion, he or she shall state in writing, under the penalties of perjury, the specific documents which are not available, the reasons the documents are not available, and what efforts have been made to obtain the documents. As more information becomes available there is a continuing duty to supplement.

TEN SUGGESTIONS AND GENERAL INFORMATION

IF YOU REPRESENT YOURSELF

READ THIS

WRITTEN BY THE BOSTON BAR ASSOCIATION
PUBLISHED BY THE SUFFOLK COUNTY PROBATE REGISTRY COMMUNITY OUTREACH PROGRAM
RICHARD IANNELLA, REGISTER

GET HELP FROM AN ATTORNEY

Generally, it is not a good idea to represent yourself. In any legal case, it is advisable to get advice and representation from an attorney.

LEGAL RESOURCES FOR LOW INCOME PARTIES

A "Lawyer for the Day" may be available to give you free help in filling out forms at the Courthouse. Check with the Register's Office about what days a "Lawyer for the Day" may be available.

The Department of Revenue (DOR), the state's child support agency, may be able to help a parent obtain child support. Custodial parents who receive public assistance automatically get free DOR services. Other parents can get an application for DOR services at the Courthouse or by calling DOR at 1-800-332-2733.

If you have trouble affording an attorney, some private attorneys may be willing to put you on a payment plan. Also, you may be eligible for free or reduced fee services from legal services programs and bar associations in your community if your income is very low.

For a list of referrals, get a copy of Legal Resources In and Around Boston from the Register's Office of the Suffolk Probate and Family Court.

TEN SUGGESTIONS IF YOU
REPRESENT YOURSELF IN COURT

5. **THINK ABOUT AND DO WHAT IS BEST FOR YOUR CHILDREN**

If your case deals with custody or visitation, think about your children's future happiness, safety and well-being. Be able to explain to the Judge why the orders that you want are best for your children.

6. **PREPARE TO GO IN FRONT OF THE JUDGE**

Think about what you will say before you go in front of the Judge; bring copies of your court papers and any other important papers. Know the dates of important things that have happened if you want to tell the Judge about those things.

The Judge is called "Your honor." Listen carefully to the Judge's questions. Try to talk to the Judge in a way that gets to the point and is clear. Be sure to tell the Judge what you want ordered and why. The person who filed the motion or started the case usually gets to speak first. The other party is given a chance to reply. Wait until it is your turn and do not interrupt the other party or the Judge. Do not lose your temper or get loud in the courtroom, even if you do not like what someone else is saying.

7. **KNOW THAT YOUR CASE MAY BE TAKEN UNDER ADVISEMENT**

The Judge may tell you what is ordered before you leave the courtroom. Sometimes a case is "taken under advisement." This means the Judge wants more time to decide the case and the Court will send you the decision once it is made. Make sure the Court has your correct mailing address.

TEN SUGGESTIONS IF YOU
REPRESENT YOURSELF IN COURT

8. **RESTRAINING ORDERS/ DOMESTIC VIOLENCE** ☆

If the other party has a history of domestic violence toward you, or if putting your address or phone number on court papers or giving this information to the other party you will put you at risk, let the courtroom Assistant Register, the court officer, and any Family Service Officer or Department of Revenue (DOR) staff involved in your case, know about any concerns for your safety. If you are sent to the Family Service Office or to DOR and you tell them that you are not comfortable with a face to face meeting with someone who has abused you, you should be interviewed separately from the person who abused you.

9. **ARRANGE FOR AN INTERPRETER IF NEEDED** 👉

If you or the other party have trouble understanding or speaking English, or are in need of a Sign Language interpreter, arrange for an interpreter for any hearing through the Register's Office of the Court as soon as you know the date of the hearing. **UNDER NO CIRCUMSTANCES SHOULD OPPOSING PARTIES INTERPRET FOR EACH OTHER.** If an interpreter is not available on the day of the hearing, the Judge may postpone the hearing to a time when an interpreter is available.

10. **GET ADVICE FROM AN ATTORNEY** ☎

Court orders often have long-lasting effects. There are likely to be rules and laws which you find hard to understand or follow without a lawyer. It is advisable that you get advice and representation from an attorney. *Probate and Family Court employees cannot give you legal advice.* If you cannot afford a lawyer, you may be eligible for free or reduced fee assistance through legal services programs or bar associations serving your community.

- 3 -

82

TEN SUGGESTIONS IF YOU
REPRESENT YOURSELF IN COURT

1. ARRIVE ON TIME FOR ANY HEARING

   If you miss the hearing, the Judge can make orders which you may not agree with even if you are not there. If you are late, your case usually takes more time.

2. DRESS IN A WAY THAT SHOWS RESPECT FOR THE COURT

   You do not need to dress like a lawyer or buy new clothes. Do, however, dress in a dignified way. Unless it is an emergency, avoid wearing jeans, T-shirts, shorts, tank-tops, sleeveless athletic shirts, cut off shirts, and undershirts in the courtroom.

3. FILL IN AND CHECK EVERY LINE OF YOUR FINANCIAL STATEMENT

   Your Financial Statement is one of the most important documents in your case. You are required to exchange copies of Financial Statements with the other party at least 2 days before the hearing on temporary orders or "pretrial" conference. Get the form well before the hearing so you have all the information you need to fill it out. You can be sent to jail for deliberately putting down false information.

4. SIGN AN AGREEMENT ONLY IF YOU CAN LIVE WITH IT

   You should not sign an agreement (also called a *stipulation*) unless you agree to do what it says. Make sure any written agreement contains your understanding of what was agreed upon and ask for a copy of it. Often if the Judge finds that the agreement is fair and reasonable, the Judge will make the agreement an order of the Court. If you do not reach an agreement, the Judge will decide your case.

- 1 -

83

TABLE OF CONTENTS

COMMON LEGAL TERMS

Affidavit of Indigency: This is a sworn statement filed by people who are poor, often to get filing fees waived and to have the state pay for the costs of having a process server "serve" the court papers on an opposing party in their case.

Alimony: Support paid to someone you are legally married to or who you were legally married to in the past.

Answer: A court case starts with a complaint filed by a plaintiff. A defendant usually has 20 days (after being served with a complaint) to file a written answer in court admitting or denying each paragraph of the complaint.

Assistant Register: Often this is the person that you check in with when you go to the courtroom where your case will be heard by a Judge. An Assistant Register assists the Judge in the courtroom and helps to process court papers in the Register's Office.

Child Support Guidelines: This is the formula that the Judge uses to set a child support order. It is based mostly on the ages of children, the number of children, and income of the parties.

Citation: In a child guardianship case, a "citation" is the form that must be "served" on the parents or other parties to the case to give notice of the case when the parents or the other parties have not signed their "assent" (meaning that they agree) to the guardianship.

Complaint: A court case is started with a complaint. The type of complaint which is best for you depends on what you want from the court and will depend on your relationship to the other party in the case. Unmarried parents often file paternity or Chapter 209C complaints; married parties often file divorce or separate support complaints.

Court Officers: Court officers are in the courthouse to keep the peace and to provide for the safety of Judges, court staff and the public. Court officers usually wear uniforms.

COMMON LEGAL TERMS

Custody: See Physical Custody, Shared Legal Custody, Sole Custody.

Defendant: The person who files the complaint is usually called the plaintiff and the other party is usually called the defendant.

Divorce: A divorce complaint is filed to legally end a marriage and to deal with division of marital property, debts, support, and children.

Docket Number: Every court case is given a number. This is on the upper right corner of most court papers.

DOR: DOR (the Department of Revenue) is the state child support agency and is involved in cases if a party or the child have received public assistance. DOR is involved in other cases if the child support is paid through DOR or a person seeking support applies for DOR services.

Family Service Officer: The Family Service Officer meets with you to see what your case is about and to try to help you reach a written agreement with the other party on the day of your hearing. The Family Service Officer is not a Judge and usually not a lawyer; he or say can repeat what you say to the Judge. The Judge also can order that the Family Service Office do a more detailed investigation of your case.

Financial Statement: You will have to fill out this form describing your financial situation if your case involves issues of support or other financial matters.

Your Financial Statement is one of the most important documents in your case. Do not wait until the last minute to fill it out. Be sure to attach copies of your W-2's and 1099 tax forms from the prior year to the Financial Statement.

84

Income Assignment: The Judge makes an order for an immediate or a suspended (inactive) income assignment whenever child support is ordered. If the order is immediate, the employer (or other source of income) is sent a copy of the order requiring that the child support be taken out of a paycheck (or other source of income) starting immediately. A suspended order can be changed to an immediate assignment if a parent gets behind in support payments.

Judgment: Cases usually start with temporary orders. After a trial or a written agreement of the parties for final resolution of the case, a judgment is entered. Usually, a judgment cannot be changed without a substantial change of circumstances.

Judgment of Divorce Nisi: After the judgment nisi enters at a divorce hearing, the divorce becomes final in 90 days.

Marking a Motion: This means scheduling a hearing on a motion. A motion is used to request temporary orders until the Court enters a final judgment or further temporary orders. Unless there is a dire emergency, a motion cannot be marked until the complaint and summons are served.

Modification: A complaint for modification is needed to start a Court case to change a judgment of the Court. (See judgment above). Motions to change temporary orders may be filed while a case is pending, but the Judge often does not modify (change) the temporary orders until trial unless things have changed in a major way since the last Court order.

Paternity cases: Cases involving parents who have children but who have not been married to each other. Also called "Chapter 209C" cases.

Physical Custody: Physical custody means who the child lives with.

Plaintiff: The person who files the complaint is called the plaintiff.

Process Server: The complaint and summons have to be served (delivered) on a defendant. Deputy Sheriffs or constables are process servers who can serve a complaint, summons, or other court papers.

Proposed Order: Whenever you file a motion for temporary orders, you must file a proposed order telling the Court what you want ordered.

85

Pro Se party: If you appear in court without a lawyer, you are a "pro se" (pronounced "pro say") party--meaning you represent yourself.

Return of Service: A summons and complaint have to be "served." The return of service is the part of the summons filled in by a Deputy Sheriff or other person who served the papers describing how service was made.

Separate Support case: A married person may file this complaint if he or she does not want a divorce, but wants to live separately from a spouse and needs support or child custody orders. (A married person seeking only support may also file a complaint for support).

Shared Legal Custody: This means both parents make decisions together on major issues relating to their child such as education, medical treatment, religion, and other important issues in the child's life. If a parent has sole legal custody, he or she can make the important decisions about the child without getting input from the other parent.

Shared Legal Custody with Physical Custody to One Parent: This means the child lives with one parent, but both parents make important decisions about the child together.

Shared Legal and Shared Physical Custody: This means the child spends substantial time living with both parents and the parents make important decisions about the child together.

Sole Custody (Sole Legal and Sole Physical Custody): This means the child lives with one parent who is solely responsible for making major decisions about the child and for the child's general upbringing.

Stipulations: Written agreements filed in Court cases.

Summons: After a complaint is filed, a summons will be issued so that the defendant can receive official notice of the case. Copies of the summons and complaint must be "served" on the defendant in the case.

Visitation order: This is a Court order that sets out when the parent who does not have physical custody can spend time with the child.

NOTES ABOUT YOUR CASE

Usually it is helpful to keep notes about what happens every time you go to court. Write down the date of the hearing, the name of the Judge, and what the Judge ordered. Make sure you get copies of and understand any orders made in your case.

> This booklet does not constitute legal advice which only can be given to you by your attorney. Every case is different. The facts of your case are important in deciding what to file in Court and how best to present your case. Get help from an attorney whenever possible.

🖐 LEGAL ROAD MAP FOR MOST DIVORCE, SEPARATE SUPPORT OR PATERNITY CASES

o A complaint and related paperwork are filed in court.

o A summons is issued.

o Defendant is served copies of the complaint and summons.

o The defendant's answer to the complaint is due 20 days from the date that the defendant is served with the complaint.

o Either party files a motion for temporary orders with a proposed order and gets a hearing date on the motion.

o The motion and proposed order are usually served by mailing it to other party at least 10 days before the hearing with notice of the place, date, and time of the hearing. 7 days notice is adequate if you hand-deliver the papers to the other party before 4 p.m.; 8 days notice is required if papers are hand-delivered after 4 p.m.

o A Judge makes temporary orders.

o After a pretrial request is made, a pretrial is scheduled to see what parties agree on and if the case can be settled without a trial.

o A Judge enters a judgment after a trial or after the parties reach an agreement for final resolution of their legal claims.

o A modification of the orders contained in the judgment usually is not obtained by either party unless there is a substantial change of circumstances or the parties both agree to change the judgment and the Court approves the change.

Parents after Separation

Guidelines for Visitation

Introduction

A separation from your spouse does not end your responsibility as a parent. Each parent should make every attempt to play a vital role in the lives of his or her children. Your children need the ongoing affection, interest and concern of a loving parent. Children should understand and feel that their parents still love them in spite of the fact that their parents could not live happily with each other. You should not travel the road to self-pity, living in the past, nurturing bitterness and turning the children against your former marriage partner. Instead, you should reach out for the opportunities that will make your life productive, satisfying and meaningful in a positive way. The way you cope with your separation will in large part determine how your children cope with it. The guidelines in this pamphlet will assist you in helping your children cope with the separation of their parents.

Visitation

The behavior of parents has a great influence on the emotional adjustment of their children. The following visitation guidelines have been found to be helpful in achieving meaningful visitation:

A. The children should be available at the time agreed upon for the visitation. A parent who is visiting should arrive on time so as not to keep the children waiting.

B. From time to time you may need to adjust your visitation schedule. If one parent has made plans with the children or if the children themselves have made plans which conflict with the visitation rights, you should be reasonable adults and work out the problem together. The spiritual well-being, health, happiness and safety of your children should be prime considerations of both parents.

C. Not keeping a visit without notifying the other parent may be construed by the child as rejection. As soon as you realize that you will not be able to keep a scheduled visit, you should notify the other parent immediately. Not to do so will cause inconvenience to your child as well as to the other parent and prevent either of them from planning a different activity.

D. The visit should not be used to check on the other parent. The children should not be pumped for this kind of information. They should not be used as spies. Often in the

Guidelines for parents

A. Allow yourself and your children time for readjustment. Convalescence from the emotional trauma of a separation of parents is essential.

B. Do not let your actions or comments cause the child to think that he or she is in any way to blame for the separation of the parents. Children, especially the young ones, often mistakenly feel they have done something wrong and believe that the problems in the family are the result of their own misdeeds. Small children may feel that some action or secret wish of theirs has caused the trouble between their parents.

C. Each parent should individually assure the child that he or she is not being rejected by that parent. When discussing the separation with the children, assure them of your feelings toward them and let the other parent also express his or her own feelings.

D. Continuing anger or bitterness toward your former partner can injure your children far more than the separation itself. The feelings you show are more important than the words you use.

E. Refrain from voicing criticism of the other parent. It is difficult but absolutely essential.

F. Do not force or encourage your child to take sides. To do so encourages frustration, guilt and resentment.

G. Both parents should strive for agreement in decisions pertaining to the children, especially discipline, so that one parent is not undermining the other parent's efforts.

H. What was once important in child rearing with both parents at home is equally as important when only one is around. The guilt parents may feel about the marriage breakdown may interfere in the disciplining of the children. A child needs consistent control and direction. Over-permissiveness, or indecisive parents who leave a child at the mercy of every passing whim and impulse, interfere with the child's healthy development. Children feel more secure when limits are set. Children need and want to know quite clearly what is expected of them. They are confused when grownups seem to permit behavior which they themselves know to be wrong. Children need leadership and sometimes authority. Parents must be ready to say "No" when necessary.

child's mind, the parents hate each other, and if this belief is reinforced the child will feel uncomfortable at the time of the visitation. In his mind, if he does anything to please the visiting parent, he may invite outright rejection by his other parent. He feels he has already lost one parent and is fearful of losing the other. For this reason parents should show mutual respect for each other.

E. Do not use your visitation period as an excuse to continue arguments with your former spouse. Do not visit your children if you have been drinking.

F. Do not make extravagant promises to your children with respect to visits which you know will not take place. Such promises which are not kept result in a loss of trust and respect for you by your children.

G. Visitation should be pleasant not only for the children, but for both parents whenever possible. The visits should not take place only in the children's home. The visiting parent may wish the children to visit in his or her home overnight, or may want to plan an enjoyable outing.

H. Often the visiting parent questions where he or she will take the children on the visits and what should be planned in the way of amusement for them particularly if they are young children. Activities may add to the pleasure of a visit, but most important of all is the parent's involvement with the children. A giving of yourself is more important than material things you may give your children. The visit is one of the few times that the visiting parent has personal contact with the children and for that reason it should be a meaningful time for both the parent and the children.

I. Visitation is a time for the parent and the children to be with each other, to enjoy each other and to maintain positive relationships. Having other people participate may dilute the parent-child experience during visitation. Also, it may appear to the children that the parent does not have time for them, and that he does not care enough to give them his undivided attention during visitation.

J. After a visit, the child may be confused and have anxieties, and both parents should make every effort to discuss the problems and agree on ways to deal with them.

I. Do not attempt to buy your child's favor by presents or special treatment or by making extravagant promises you know you cannot keep.

J. Marriage breakdown is always hard on the children. They may not always show their distress or realize initially what this will mean to them. Parents should be direct and simple in telling children what is happening and why, and in a way a child can understand and digest. This will vary with the circumstances and with each child's age and comprehension. The questions asked by the child may be a key as to how much information the child is ready to absorb.

K. You should not try to hush things up and make a child feel that he must not talk or even think about what he senses is going on. Unpleasant happenings need an explanation which should be brief, timely, direct and honest. Although it would be unfortunate to present separation as a tragedy and either party as a martyr, it would also be a pity to pretend there are no regrets and that the separation of the parents is so common that it hardly matters.

L. The story of the separation of the parents may have to be retold as a child gets older and considers life more maturely.

If you need help

It is unfortunate that many people believe that to ask for help is a sign of weakness, for in reality it is a sign of strength. It takes a great deal of courage for a human being to say "I have a problem which I cannot solve alone and I need help with it." Asking for help does not mean that a person is incapable of solving his problems, for in the final analysis, it is the person himself who solves his problems.

Professional counseling may create an awareness which can assist you in dealing with your children's problems. The counselor's function is to guide the person and give some direction to his search for solution in meeting the emotional needs of the children. There is hardly a person who has not needed help at some time in his or her life. The family service officer of the probate courts in the Commonwealth of Massachusetts or an attorney may provide you with the names of professional counselors, governmental agencies or other services which will be able to assist you in dealing with problems in this area.

Commonwealth of Massachusetts
The Trial Court
Middlesex **Division**   **Probate and Family Court Department**   Docket No. _____

Joint Petition For Divorce Under M.G.L. Ch. 208, Sec. 1A

Molly Brown _____ **and** _Desmond Brown_ _____
| **Petitioner** | **Petitioner** |

of _39 Lilac Court_ _____   of _19 Leonard Avenue   Apt. 1_ _____
| (Street and No.) | (Street and No.) |

Cambridge   _MA_   _02141_   _Cambridge_   _MA_   _02139_
| (City or Town)   (State)   (Zip) | (City or Town)   (State)   (Zip) |

1. Now come the Husband and Wife in a joint petition for divorce pursuant to Massachusetts General Laws, Chapter 208, Sec. 1A.

2. The parties were lawfully married at _Concord, Massachusetts_ _____
   on _June 19, 1982_ _____ and last lived together at _Cambridge, Massachusetts_
   on _January 3, 1998_ _____ 19 _____ .

3. The minor child _____ of this marriage and date(s) of birth is/are:

   Stephen, born August 12, 1983 _____   _____

   Michael, born August 18, 1989 _____   _____

4. The parties certify that no previous action for divorce, annulment, affirmation of marriage, separate support, desertion, living apart for justifiable cause, or custody of child _____ has been brought by either party against the other.~~except~~ _____

5. On or about _January 3_ _____ , 19 _98_ ____ , an irretrievable breakdown of the marriage under M.G.L. Ch. 208, Sec. 1A occurred and continues to exist.

6. Wherefore, the parties pray that the Court:
   - ☒ grant a divorce on the ground of irretrievable breakdown
   - ☒ approve the separation agreement executed by the parties
   - ☐ incorporate and merge said agreement executed by the parties
   - ☒ incorporate but not merge said agreement, which shall survive and remain as an independent contract,
   - ☒ allow Wife to resume her former name of _Molly Jones_   _except for provisions which_
   - ☐ _____   _relate to the children._

Date _October 19, 1998_ _____   _October 21, 1998_

Molly Brown   _Desmond Brown_
SIGNATURE OF WIFE ~~OR ATTORNEY~~   SIGNATURE OF HUSBAND ~~OR ATTORNEY~~

(Print address if not pro se)   (Print address if not pro se)

_____   _____

Tel. No. (_617_) _494-2439_   Tel. No. (_617_) _494-8731_

B.B.O. # _____   B.B.O. # _____

89

Joint Petition for Divorce
Under M.G.L. c. 208, Sec. 1A

For Wife:

Molly Brown

Address 39 Lilac Court

Cambridge MA   02141

Tel No. (617)   494-2439

For Husband:

Desmond Brown

Address 19 Leonard Avenue, Apt. 1

Cambridge MA   02139

Tel. No. (617)   494-8731

Docket No. _____

Filed _____ 19 ____

Agreement Approved _____ 19 ____

Judgment _____ 19 ____

Documents filed:

Marriage Certificate	☒
Wife's Financial Statement	☒
Husband's Financial Statement	☒
Separation Agreement	☒
Affidavit of Irretrievable Breakdown	☒
Affidavit Disclosing Care or Custody Proceedings	☒
Child Support Guidelines Worksheet	☒

COMMONWEALTH OF MASSACHUSETTS

Middlesex Division

Probate and Family Court
No.

MOLLY BROWN, Joint Petitioner

v.

AFFIDAVIT OF IRRETRIEVABLE

BREAKDOWN OF MARRIAGE

DESMOND BROWN, Joint Petitioner

We, MOLLY BROWN and DESMOND BROWN make this affidavit in support of our joint petition for divorce, pursuant to Massachusetts General Laws, Chapter 208, Section 1A, and state as follows:

1. An irretrievable breakdown of our marriage exists, in that there have arisen between us differences in goals, and philosophies too deep to be reconciled.
2. We have not lived together since January 3, 1998.
3. We are both certain that our marriage is no longer viable.

Sworn to under pains and penalties of perjury this 21st day of October, 1998.

Molly Brown 10-19-98   _Desmond Brown_
Molly Brown   Desmond Brown

COMMONWEALTH OF MASSACHUSETTS

Middlesex County   October 19, 1998

Then personally appeared the above-named MOLLY BROWN, who executed the foregoing instrument and who acknowledged that she executed the same as her free act and deed, before me

Banks Teller
Notary Public
My Commission Expires: 11-23-2003

COMMONWEALTH OF MASSACHUSETTS

Middlesex County   October 21, 1998

Then personally appeared the above-named DESMOND BROWN, who executed the foregoing instrument and who acknowledged that he executed the same as his free act and deed, before me

Banks Teller
Notary Public
My Commission Expires: 11-23-2003

<table>
<tr><td>AFFIDAVIT DISCLOSING CARE OR CUSTODY PROCEEDINGS
Pursuant to Trial Court Rule IV</td><td colspan="2">TRIAL COURT OF MASSACHUSETTS
Name Of Case — Joint Petition for Divorce of
Molly Brown and Desmond Brown</td><td>DOCKET NUMBER</td></tr>
</table>

☐ Boston Municipal Court	☐ District Court ___ Division	☐ Juvenile Court ___ Division	☒ Probate & Family Court Middlesex Division	☐ Superior Court ___ Division

Section 1

I, _Molly Brown_ , hereby declare, to the best of
NAME OF PARTY (PRINT)
my knowledge, information, and belief that all the information on this form is true and complete:

Section 2

The name(s) of the child(ren) whose care or custody is at issue in this case are:

A. _Brown, Stephen_   B. _Brown, Michael_   C. _____
(LAST, FIRST)   (LAST, FIRST)   (LAST, FIRST)

Use only the letter appearing in front of the child's name above when referring to that child in completing the remaining sections.

Section 3

The party filing this affidavit may request certain addresses to be kept confidential if the address is a shelter for battered persons and their dependent child(ren), **or** the party filing this affidavit believes that he/she or the child(ren) are in danger of physical or emotional abuse, **or** the party is filing an action under G.L.c.209A. **If you believe that this provision applies to you, check the box at the right, complete sections 10 and 11 on the reverse side of this page and DO NOT complete sections 4 and 5 below.** ☐

Section 4

The address(es) of the above-named child(ren) whose care or custody is at issue in this case are:

Address(es)   Address(es) During Last 2 Years, If Different

CHILD A. _39 Lilac Court, Cambridge MA 02141_ _____

CHILD B. _39 Lilac Court, Cambridge MA 02141_ _____

CHILD C. _____

Section 5

My address is: _39 Lilac Court, Cambridge MA 02141_ _____

Section 6

I ☐ have ☒ have not participated in and I ☐ **know** ☒ **do not know** of other care or custody proceedings involving the above-named child(ren) in Massachusetts or in any other state or country.

Certified copies of any pleadings or determinations in a care or custody proceeding outside of Massachusetts listed in sections 7 and 8 must be filed with this affidavit unless already filed with this court or an extension for filing these documents has been granted by this court.

Section 7

The following is a list of all pending or concluded proceedings I have participated in or know of involving the care or custody of the above-named child(ren):

Letter of Child	Court	Docket No.	Status of Case (Custody awarded to) (Date of award)	[W]itness [P]arty [O]ther [N]one
CHILD ___	_____	_____	_____	[ ]
CHILD ___	_____	_____	_____	[ ]
CHILD ___	_____	_____	_____	[ ]

Section 8

The names and addresses of parties to care or custody proceedings involving any of the above-named child(ren) or those claiming a legal right to these child(ren) during the last two years (not including myself) are:

Letter of Child	Name of Party/Claimant	Current (or last known) Address of Party/Claimant
CHILD ___	_____	_____
CHILD ___	_____	_____
CHILD ___	_____	_____

Section 9

If the box at the right is checked, this affidavit discloses the adoption of one or more of the above-named child(ren) and I am requesting the court to impound this affidavit. See instructions. ☐

This affidavit must be personally signed by the party listed in section 1 above, unless he/she is under 18 years of age or has been adjudged incompetent in which case the attorney of record must sign. A revised affidavit must be filed with the court if new information is discovered subsequent to this filing.

Signed this _19th_ day of _October_ ,19 _98_ under the penalties of perjury.

X _Molly Brown_
SIGNATURE OF PARTY OR ATTORNEY OF RECORD FOR INCOMPETENT/JUVENILE

Molly Brown
PRINTED NAME OF PERSON SIGNING

92

_____
ADDRESS OF ATTORNEY OF RECORD FOR INCOMPETENT/JUVENILE

THE PARTY FILING THIS AFFIDAVIT MUST FURNISH A COPY OF IT TO ALL OTHER PARTIES TO THIS ACTION.

CAJ-1 TCR IV (7/95)

Commonwealth of Massachusetts
The Trial Court

Middlesex Division   **Probate and Family Court Department**   Docket No._____

Financial Statement
(SHORT FORM)

Molly Brown   v.   Desmond Brown
Plaintiff/Petitioner   Defendant/ Petitioner

INSTRUCTIONS: If your income equals or exceeds $75,000.00 you must complete the LONG FORM financial statement, unless otherwise ordered by the Court. All questions on both sides of this form must be answered in full or the word "none" inserted. If additional space is needed for any answer, an attached sheet may be filed in addition to, but not in lieu of, the answer. Information contained herein is confidential and only available to the parties and persons authorized under Probate and Family Court Department Supplemental Rule 401.

1. Your Name Molly Brown   Soc. Sec. No. 029-49-4492
   Address   39 Lilac Street   Cambridge   MA   02141
                (street and no.)   (city or town)   (state)   (zip)

   Age 39 Tel. No.(617) 494-2439   No. of Children living with you 2
   Occupation sales   Employer Trident Restaurant and Bookstore
   Employer's Address   338 Newbury Street   Boston   MA
                        (street and no.)   (city or town)   (state)   (zip)

   Employer's Tel. No. (617) 267-8688   Health Ins. Coverage [X]YES [ ]NO
   Health Insurance Provider Blue Cross - Blue Shield   Cert. No. _____

2. **Gross Weekly Income from All Sources (strike inapplicable words)**
   a). Base pay from salary, wages _____ $ 558.00
   b). Self Employment Income **(attach a completed Schedule A)** _____ $ --
   c). Income from overtime-commissions-tips-bonuses-part-time job _____ $ --
   d). Dividends - interest _____ $ --
   e). Income from trusts or annuities _____ $ --
   f). Pensions and retirement funds _____ $ --
   g). Social Security _____ $ --
   h). Disability, unemployment insurance or worker's compensation _____ $ --
   i). Public Assistance (welfare, A.F.D.C. payments) _____ $ --
   j). Rental from Income Producing Property **(attach a completed Schedule B)** ___ $ --
   k). All other sources (including child support, alimony) _____ $ 217.00

   l). **Total Gross Weekly Income** (a through k) $ 775.00

3. **Itemize Deductions from Gross Income**
   a). Federal income tax deductions (claiming __1__ exemptions) _____ $ 45.45
   b). State income tax deductions (claiming __1__ exemptions) _____ $ 23.41
   c). F.I.C.A./Medicare _____ $ 22.19
   d). Medical Insurance _____ $ --
   e). Union Dues _____ $ --

   f). **Total Deductions** (a through e) **$** 91.05

4. **Adjusted Net Weekly Income**
   2 (l) minus 3 (f) _____ $ 683.95

5. **Other Deductions from Salary**
   a). Credit Union (Loan Repayment or Savings) _____ $ --
   b). Savings _____ $ 50.00
   c). Retirement _____ $ 50.00
   d). Other - Specify (such as Deferred Compensation or 401K) _____ $ --

   e). **Total Deductions** (a through d) **$** 100.00

6. **Net Weekly Income**   4 minus 5 (e) $ 583.95

7. **Gross Yearly Income from Prior Year** _____ $ 28,500
   (attach copy of all W-2 and 1099 forms for prior year)

93

CJ-D 301S (11/97)

8. **Weekly Expenses** (Do Not Duplicate Weekly Expenses - Strike Inapplicable Words)
   a) Rent - Mortgage (PIT) $ 130.   l) Life Insurance $ 2.
   b) Homeowner's/Tenant Insurance $ 10.   m) Medical Insurance $ --
   c) Maintenance and Repair $ 5.   n) Uninsured Medicals $ 15.
   d) Heat (Type_____) $ 25.   o) Incidentals and Toiletries $ 10.
   e) Electricity and/or Gas $ 15.   p) Motor Vehicle Expenses $ 35.
   f) Telephone $ 10.   q) Motor Vehicle Loan Payment $ 48.
   g) Water/Sewer $ 12.   r) Child Care $ 100.
   h) Food $ 100.   s) Other (attach additional schedule, if necessary) $ _____
   i) House Supplies $ 10.   _____ $ _____
   j) Laundry and Cleaning $ 5.   _____ $ _____
   k) Clothing $ 50.

   Total Weekly Expenses (a through s) $ 582.

9. **Counsel Fees**
   a) Retainer amount(s) paid to your attorney(s) $ _____
   b) Legal fees incurred, to date, against retainer(s) $ _____
   c) Anticipated range of total legal expense to prosecute this action $ _____ to $ _____

10. **Assets** (Attach additional schedule for additional real estate and other assets, if necessary)
    a) Real Estate _____
       Location   39 Lilac Court, Cambridge MA
       Title   Molly and Desmond Brown
       Fair Market Value $ 200,000 - Mortgage(s) $ 40,000 = Equity   ½ $ 80,000
    b) IRA, Keough, Pension, Profit Sharing, Other Retirement Plans
       List Financial Institution or Plan Names and Account Numbers
       Cambridge Trust, IRA #25-2647-1 $ 9,000
       _____ $ _____
       _____ $ _____
    c) Tax Deferred Annuity Plan(s) _____ $ --
    d) Life Insurance: Present Cash Value _____ $ --
    e) Savings & Checking Accounts, Money Market Accounts, and CDs - which are held
       individually, jointly, in the name of another person for your benefit, or held by you for the
       benefit of your minor child(ren). **List Financial Institution Names and Account Numbers**
       Cambridge Savings Bank #19939-2   savings $ 5,000
       Cambridge Savings Bank #0-9618632-2-8   checking $ 1,100
       _____ $ _____
    f) Motor Vehicles
       Fair Market Value $ 8,000 - Motor Vehicle Loan $ 4,000 = Equity $ 4,000
       Fair Market Value $_____ - Motor Vehicle Loan $_____ = Equity $ _____
    g) Other (such as - stocks, bonds, collections)
       _____ $ _____
       _____ $ _____

       h) **Total Assets** (a through g) $ 99,100

11. **Liabilities** (DO NOT list weekly expenses but DO list all liabilities)

	Creditor	Nature of Debt	Date of Origin	Amount Due	Weekly Payment
a)	Mastercard			$900	$10
b)					
c)					
d)					
e)	**Total Amount Due and Total Weekly Payment**		$ 900		$ 10

12. **Number of Years you have paid to Social Security**   21   yea

I certify under the penalties of perjury that my income and expenses, assets, and liabilities as stated herein are true to the
of my knowledge and belief. I have carefully read this financial statement and certify the information is true and complete
Date   June 1, 1998   Signature   Molly Brown

STATEMENT BY ATTORNEY

I, the undersigned attorney, am admitted to practice law in the Commonwealth of Massachusetts -- am admitted pro hoc vic
the purposes of this case -- and am an officer of the court. As the attorney for the party on whose behalf this Financial Statem
is submitted, I hereby state to the court that I have no knowledge that any of the information contained herein is false.

Attorney's Signature _____   Date _____
Address _____ 94 _____   Tel. No. (   ) _____
B.B.O. # _____

The Commonwealth of Massachusetts
DEPARTMENT OF PUBLIC HEALTH
REGISTRY OF VITAL RECORDS AND STATISTICS
CERTIFICATE OF ABSOLUTE
DIVORCE
(Chap. 208, Sec. 46 G.L.)
R-408

HUSBAND NAME	FIRST Desmond	MIDDLE	LAST Brown	
USUAL RESIDENCE STREET ADDRESS 2a 19 Leonard Avenue, Apt. 1		CITY TOWN OR LOCATION 2b Cambridge		
COUNTY 2c Middlesex	STATE 2d MA	DATE OF BIRTH (Mo Day Yr) 3 10-19-46	NUMBER OF THIS MARRIAGE (1st 2nd Specify) 4 1	
WIFE NAME 5a	FIRST Molly	MIDDLE Jean	LAST Brown	MAIDEN NAME 5b Jones
USUAL RESIDENCE STREET ADDRESS 6a 39 Lilac Court		CITY TOWN OR LOCATION 6b Cambridge		
COUNTY 6c Middlesex	STATE 6d MA	DATE OF BIRTH (Mo Day Yr) 7 10-21-54	NUMBER OF THIS MARRIAGE (1st 2nd Specify) 8 1	
DATE OF THIS MARRIAGE (Mo Day Yr) 9 6-19-82	NUMBER OF CHILDREN BORN ALIVE OF THIS MARRIAGE 10a 2		NUMBER OF CHILDREN UNDER AGE 18 IN THIS FAMILY 10b 2	

FOR COURT USE ONLY		
COUNTY OF JUDGMENT **MIDDLESEX s.s.** 11a	TITLE OF COURT **PROBATE & FAMILY COURT** 11a	
DATE OF JUDGMENT NISI (Mo Day Yr) 12	TYPE OF JUDGMENT DIVORCE OR ANNULMENT (Specify) 13 **DIVORCE**	DATE OF JUDGMENT ABSOLUTE (Mo Day Yr) 14
DOCKET NUMBER 15	NAME OF PLAINTIFF 16	CAUSE FOR WHICH GRANTED 17
SIGNATURE OF CERTIFYING OFFICIAL 18a	TITLE OF OFFICIAL 18b ACTING	MARIE A. GARDIN **REGISTER**

Commonwealth of Massachusetts
THE TRIAL COURT
THE PROBATE AND FAMILY COURT DEPARTMENT

_____Middlesex_____ Division   Docket No. _98D-1456_

REQUEST FOR TRIAL — ~~PRE-TRIAL~~ ASSIGNMENT
THIS FORM SHOULD **NOT** BE USED FOR MARK-UP OF TEMPORARY ORDERS AND MOTIONS
Please print or type

Please assign
for hearing: Molly Brown
                      _____
                          Joint Petitioner   ~~Plaintiff~~

                              v.

                      Desmond Brown
                      _____
                          Joint Petitioner   ~~Defendant~~

TYPE OF CASE _Divorce_____ TIME REQUIRED _10 minutes___ HEARING AT _Cambridge___

(X) Uncontested

( ) Contested

    ( ) Merits
    ( ) Custody
    ( ) Support
    ( ) Visitation
    ( ) 208, § 34
    ( ) Other_____

The following papers must be on file before
cases can be assigned for hearing:

( ) Summons or Return of Service
(X) Marriage Certificate
(X) Statistical Form R408
(X) Financial Statement (Supp. Rule 401)
(X) Affidavits of Both Parties (1A Divorces)
(X) Notarized Agreement (1A Divorces)
(X) Affidavit Disclosing Care and Custody

Has Discovery Been Completed (X) Yes ( ) No

Has This Case Been Pre-Tried ( ) Yes (X) No

I hereby certify that, in my opinion, this case is ready for trial.

Requested by: Opposing Counsel:

____Molly Brown_____   Name   __Desmond Brown_____
____39 Lilac Court, Cambridge MA 02141__ Address __19 Leonard Ave., Apt. 1, Cambridge__
                                          and
____(617) 494-2439_____   Phone No. _(617) 494-8731_____ MA 02139

- -

FOR REGISTER'S USE ONLY
ACTION

The above-entitled matter has been assigned for

_____ (Trial) _____ (Pre-Trial Conference

at _____ on _____ 19____, at _____

_____ . Returned without action. Data Incomplete. See above.
                                        96

                                                        _____
                                                        | |
                                                        |_____|
                                                        Clerk's Initials

Register of Probate
1/82

Commonwealth of Massachusetts
The Trial Court
Norfolk Division   **Probate and Family Court Department**   Docket No._____

Complaint For Divorce

Elizabeth Beauchamp _____, Plaintiff

v.

Edward Beauchamp _____, Defendant

1. Plaintiff, who resides at 39 Elm Street   Dedham   Norfolk   MA   02026
   (Street and No.)   (City or Town)   (County)   (State)   (Zip)

   was lawfully married to the defendant who now resides at 39 Elm Street
   (Street and No.)

   Dedham   Norfolk   MA   02026
   (City or Town)   (County)   (State)   (Zip)

2. The parties were married at Walpole MA _____ on July 1, 1981
   and last lived together at Dedham _____ on _____
       and continue to live together at Dedham

3. The minor child ren _____ of this marriage, and date(s) of birth is/are:
   Catherine, born October 15, 1987
   Margaret, born January 25, 1989
   George, born May 12, 1992

4. Plaintiff certifies that no previous action for divorce, annulling or affirming marriage, separate support, desertion, living apart for justifiable cause, or custody of child _____ has been brought by either party against the other, except:
   _____
   _____

5. On or about January 19 _____, 19 98 _____, the defendant committed acts of cruel and abusive treatment against me, as he has done on numerous other occasions.
   _____
   _____
   _____

6. Wherefore, plaintiff requests that the Court:
   ☒ grant a divorce for cruel and abusive treatment
   ☒ prohibit defendant from imposing any restraint on plaintiff's personal liberty
   ☒ grant him/her custody of the above-named children
   ☒ order a suitable amount for support of the plaintiff and said minor child ren
   ☒ order conveyance of the real estate located at 39 Elm Street, Dedham, Massachusetts
   _____ standing in the name of Edward Beauchamp and
   Elizabeth Beauchamp _____ as recorded with Norfolk County
   Registry of Deeds, Book 21798 _____ Page 434
   ☐ allow plaintiff to resume her former name of _____
   ☒ order such other relief as shall seem just

Date January 21, 1998   *Elizabeth Beauchamp*
         Signature of ~~Attorney or~~ Plaintiff, if pro se

Print name and address Elizabeth Beauchamp

97

39 Elm Street, Dedham MA 02026

Tel. No. (781) 326-2711 B.B.O. # _____

CJ-D 101 (6/90)

Complaint For Divorce

For Plaintiff:

Elizabeth Beauchamp

Address 39 Elm Street

Dedham MA 02026

Tel. No. (781) 326-2711

For Defendant:

H. A. Lincoln, Jr., Esq.

Address 575 Moody Street

Waltham MA 02154

Tel. No. (781) 899-7548

Docket No. _____

Filed _____ 19 _____

Judgment _____ 19 _____

Temporary Orders _____ 19 _____

_____

_____

_____

Documents filed:

Marriage Certificate   ☒

Plaintiff's Financial Statement   ☒

Defendant's Financial Statement   ☐

Service on Summons   ☒

Affidavit Disclosing Care or   ☒
Custody Proceedings

Instructions

Refer to Massachusetts General Laws Chapter 208 and Massachusetts Rules of Domestic Relations Procedure.

1) A certified copy of your civil marriage certificate must be filed with this Complaint.

2) Recite street address, city or town, and county in paragraphs one and two; city or town and county or state in paragraph five.

3) In completing paragraph four, please provide only the docket number and county.

4) The allegations in paragraph five must comply with General Laws Chapter 208, Section 1 and 2 and Massachusetts Rules of Domestic Relations Procedure Rule 8.

5) Affidavit Disclosing Care or Custody Proceedings must be filed with this complaint pursuant to Trial Court Rule IV identifying the minor child(ren) of this marriage.

6) All requests for temporary relief must be made by motion, although several prayers may be contained in one. For temporary restraining orders see Mass. R. Dom. Rel. P. Rule 65, affidavit requirement.

7) If attachment or trustee process is desired, a motion with affidavit must be filed. A certificate of insurance is normally not required in domestic relations cases. See Massachusetts Rules of Domestic Relations Procedures Rules 4.1 and 4.2.

8) Plaintiff must sign this Complaint if appearing pro se; otherwise plaintiff's attorney must sign and give his/her address in the space provided.

__Norfolk___ **Division**   **Probate and Family Court Department**   **Docket No.** _98D-7579___

Domestic Relations Summons

_____ Elizabeth Beauchamp _____ , **Plaintiff**

v.

_____ Edward Beauchamp _____ , **Defendant**

To the above named Defendant:

You are hereby summoned and required to serve upon _Elizabeth Beauchamp_____

plaintiff's attorney whose address is __39 Elm Street, Dedham MA 02026_____

_____ a copy of your answer to the complaint for ___divorce____
                                                                      (type of action)

which is herewith served upon you, within 20 days after service of this summons upon you, exclusive of the day of service. If you fail to do so, the Court will proceed to the hearing and adjudication of this action. You are also required to file your answer to the complaint in the office of the Register of this Court at _____Dedham_____ either before service upon plaintiff's attorney or within a reasonable time thereafter.

Witness ___████████████_____ **DAVID H. KOPELMAN**_____ Esquire, First Justice of said Court

at _____Dedham_____ , this _____21st_____ day of

_____January_____ , 19_98___ .

_____Thomas Patrick Hughes_____
Register of Probate

ACCEPTANCE OF SERVICE

I, _____ , the above named Defendant hereby accept service of this summons and understand that judgment may be rendered against me in accordance with the complaint a copy of which I have received this day.

Date _____

_____
                       Signature of Defendant

NOTARIZATION

_____ ss   Date _____

Then personally appeared the above named _____

who made oath that the foregoing acceptance was his free act and deed.

Signature of Notary Public _____

99   Print Name _____

My Commission Expires _____

CJ-D 110 (1/89)

Commonwealth of Massachusetts
The Trial Court
Probate and Family Court Department

__Norfolk__ Division

Docket No. _98D-7579_

Proof Of Service

I hereby certify and return that on _____ , 19 _____ , I served a copy of the within summons, together with a copy of the complaint in this action upon the within named defendant by _____

_____

~~in the presence of ~~_____ ~~of~~ _____
~~who identified said defendant (italics applicable to Divorce Complaint only).~~

Date _____

Signed under the penalties of perjury.

Date of Service _____

_____
Signature of officer or other server.

~~Affidavit Of Identifying Witness (Applicable In Divorce Action Only)~~

I, _____ , of _____
hereby certify that I personally know the defendant named herein, that the defendant is the spouse of the plaintiff and was served with a copy of this summons together with a copy of complaint for divorce in my presence on

_____ , 19 _____ , at _____
(street and number)

_____
(city or town)   (county)   (state)   (zip)

Signed under the penalties of perjury.

Date _____   _____

Proof Of Service Of Disinterested Server
Who Is Also Identifying Witness
(Applicable In Divorce Actions Only)

I, ___Joan Neighbors___ , of _37 Elm Street, Dedham MA_____
hereby certify that I personally know the defendant named herein, that the defendant is the spouse of the plaintiff and was served with a copy of this summons together with a copy of complaint for divorce on _January 21_ , 19 _98_ ,
at ___39 Elm Street_____
(street and number)

___Dedham___   ___Norfolk___   __MA__   _02026_
(city or town)   (county)   (state)   (zip)

Signed under the penalties of perjury.

Joan Neighbors

Date _January 21, 1998_   100   _____

Note: The signature of the defendant must be notarized by a disinterested notary or justice of the peace who is neither associated in business with nor employed by the plaintiff or his attorney.

Note: Service of process must comply with Massachusetts Rules of Domestic Relations Procedure Rule 4.

Commonwealth of Massachusetts
The Trial Court

__Norfolk__ **Division**   **Probate and Family Court Department**   **Docket No.** _____

__Elizabeth Beauchamp_____
Plaintiff/Petitioner

v.

MOTION FOR

__Emergency Vacate, Restraining__

__Edward Beauchamp_____
Defendant/Respondent

__and Custody Orders__

Now comes____Elizabeth Beauchamp_____ , the plaintiff/defendant/petitioner/respondent,
(name of moving party)

in this action who moves this Honorable Court as follows: ___to order that_____

__(1) Defendant vacate the marital home at 39 Elm Street, Dedham,__

__(2) Defendant be restrained from interfering with Plaintiff's liberty, and__

__(3) Plaintiff have temporary legal and physical custody of the minor children,__

__Catherine age 10, Margaret age 8 and George age 5. I have not given__

__Defendant notice of this motion for fear of further abuse.__

NOTICE OF HEARING

This Motion will be heard at the Probate & Family

Court in _____
(city)

on _____
(month/day/year)

at _____
(time of hearing)

Elizabeth Beauchamp
(signature)

Elizabeth Beauchamp
(PRINT name)

39 Elm Street
(street address)

Dedham MA   02026
(city or town)   (state)   (zip code)

Date: __January 21, 1998_____   Tel. No. (781)___326-2623_____

The within motion is hereby **ALLOWED — DENIED.**

_____

_____

_____

_____

Date   Justice of the Probate and Family Court

101

INSTRUCTIONS

1. <u>Generally,</u> refer to Mass.R.Civ.P./Mass.R.Dom.Rel.P. 6 and 7; Probate Court Rules 6, 29, and 29B.
2. If the opposing party is represented by an attorney who has filed an appearance, service of this motion <u>MUST</u> be made on the attorney.
3. Certificate of Service on Reverse side must be completed.

CJ-D 400 (8/96)

COMMONWEALTH OF MASSACHUSETTS

Norfolk Division

Probate and Family Court

No.

ELIZABETH BEAUCHAMP, Plaintiff

v.

EDWARD BEAUCHAMP, Defendant

PLAINTIFF'S AFFIDAVIT IN SUPPORT OF HER MOTION FOR EMERGENCY VACATE, RESTRAINING AND CUSTODY ORDERS

On Monday January 19 about 8 p.m. my husband came home drunk again. He started to insult me and to shout at the children, who were watching TV downstairs. Then my husband threw a glass ashtray at the TV. It missed and shattered against the wall. The children were very scared and George, age 5, started to cry. I took him upstairs to his bedroom and also asked Margaret and Catherine to go to bed.

Mr. Beauchamp followed me up to George's room and kicked open the door, which was not locked. He pushed me up against the wall and tried to strangle me. George screamed and the girls ran into the room. Then he let go.

The children and I were afraid to sleep in the house that night so we went to the house of a friend in Westwood, where we have stayed the past two days.

My husband has had a drinking problem for several years. He has been increasingly abusive in the last few months. He refuses to go for help or even to admit that he has a problem. Often he does not remember what he has done.

I need immediate protective orders because my health and safety and that of the children are threatened by my husband's abusive conduct.

Signed under pains and penalties of perjury, this 21st day of January, 1998.

Elizabeth Beauchamp
Elizabeth Beauchamp

102

COMMONWEALTH OF MASSACHUSETTS

THE TRIAL COURT

PROBATE AND FAMILY COURT DEPARTMENT

NORFOLK DIVISION

Elizabeth Beauchamp	MOTION TO FILE MARRIAGE
PLAINTIFF	CERTIFICATE LATE
v.	
Edward Beauchamp	
DEFENDENT	

Now comes the plaintiff and asks that he/she be allowed to file this action without filing a marriage certificate at this time. He/She affirms that the marriage certificate is not available because: of insufficient time to obtain it before filing emergency motions.

He/She further states that he/she will file a certified copy of the marriage certificate with this Court forthwith.

Respectfully submitted,

January 21, 1998

Name: _Elizabeth Beauchamp_

Address: _39 Elm Street_

City or Town _Dedham MA 02026_

Date: _January 21, 1998_

The above motion is hereby denied – allowed.

_____
Justice, Probate And Family Court

103

IH-66

__Norfolk__ **Division**   **Probate and Family Court Department**   Docket No. _98D-7579_

Elizabeth Beauchamp
_____
Plaintiff/Petitioner

v.

Edward Beauchamp
_____
Defendant/Respondent

MOTION FOR

Temporary Restraining Order to
_____

Preserve Marital Assets
_____

Now comes _Elizabeth Beauchamp_ , the plaintiff/defendant/petitioner/respondent,
(name of moving party)

in this action who moves this Honorable Court as follows: _to issue a temporary restraining_

order to preserve the following marital assets pending a final hearing on the

merits of plaintiff's Complaint for Divorce.

(1) Dedham Savings Bank joint savings (235790458) ($15,400)

(2) Niagara Falls (AB-1505-2) joint securities ($34,000)

(3) Raytheon Fund (03457-A1) pension ($98,000)

(4) Bulworth Mutual (25-63-478) life insurance ($100,000)

without notice to defendant, as per my Affidavit of Irreparable Harm, attached.

Elizabeth Beauchamp
(signature)

The within motion is hereby
ALLOWED — DENIED.

_____   _____
Date   Justice of the Probate and Family Court

Elizabeth Beauchamp
(PRINT name)

39 Elm Street
(street address)

Dedham   _MA_   _02026_
(city or town)   (state)   (zip code)

Tel. No. (_781_) _326-2711_

Date:_ February 17, 1998_

NOTICE OF HEARING

This Motion will be heard at the Probate and Family Court in _____
(city)

on _____ at _____.
(month/day/year)   (time of hearing)

CERTIFICATE OF SERVICE

I hereby certify that I have served a copy of this motion upon:

_____

(name of party and address or name and address of attorney of record; including, street address/city or town/zip code)

_____

by — delivery in hand on _____ — mailing (postage paid) on
(date of delivery)

_____ . 104 _____
(date of mailing)   (signature)

INSTRUCTIONS

1. Generally, refer to Mass.R.Civ.P./Mass.R.Dom.Rel.P. 6 and 7; Probate Court Rules 6, 29, and 29B.

2. If the opposing party is represented by an attorney who has filed an appearance, service of this motion MUST be made on the attorney.

CJ-D 400 (10/93)

COMMONWEALTH OF MASSACHUSETTS
THE TRIAL COURT
THE PROBATE AND FAMILY COURT DEPARTMENT

NORFOLK DIVISION

DOCKET NO. 98D-7579

AFFIDAVIT OF IRREPARABLE HARM

I, _____Elizabeth Beauchamp_____ affirm

that prior notice to said _____Edward Beauchamp_____ would

result in irreparable harm if the within motion is not immediately granted by this

court because: there is a strong likelihood that my husband will further

deplete our marital assets before the entry of a temporary restraining

order if he is given prior notice.

I have just found out that he withdrew $12,000 from our account

at Dedham Savings without my knowledge or consent.

Date _February 17, 1998_____   _Elizabeth Beauchamp_____

Signed under penalties of perjury

105

IH-40

Commonwealth of Massachusetts
The Trial Court
Probate and Family Court Department

Norfolk Division

Docket No. 98D-7579

Elizabeth Beauchamp ,
          Plaintiff

v.

Edward Beauchamp ,
          Defendant

MOTION FOR

Temporary Child Support

Pursuant to Guidelines

Now comes ___Elizabeth Beauchamp___ , the plaintiff/defendant/petitioner, in this
          (name of moving party)

action who moves this Honorable Court as follows: __to order defendant to pay__

__child support pursuant to the guidelines for the 3 minor children of__

__the marriage, Catherine born 10-15-87, Margaret born 1-25-89 and__

__George born 5-12-92.__

DATE February 17, 1998

The within motion is hereby
ALLOWED/DENIED.

_____   _____
Date   Justice of the Probate and Family Court

Elizabeth Beauchamp
(signature)
Elizabeth Beauchamp
(PRINT NAME)
39 Elm Street
(street address)
Dedham MA 02026
(city or town/state/zip code)
(781) 326-2711
(telephone number)

NOTICE OF HEARING

This Motion will be heard at the Probate and Family Court in ____Dedham____
                                                        (city)

on ___March 4, 1998___ at ___8:30 a.m.___ .
     (month/day/year)   (time of hearing)

CERTIFICATE OF SERVICE

I hereby certify that I have served on this date a copy of this motion upon:

__Edward Beauchamp, 28 Old Road, Franklin MA 02038 by mailing copies of this__
        (Name of party and address, including street address/city or town/zip code)

__motion to him by first class and certified mail__
by delivery in hand/mailing (postage paid).

__February 17, 1998__   *Elizabeth Beauchamp*
(Date)   (Signature)

INSTRUCTIONS
106
1. Generally, refer to Mass.R.Dom.Rel.P. 6 and 7.
2. Please return the completed certificate of service to the Probate Court before the hearing of this Motion.

IH-3

Commonwealth of Massachusetts

NORFOLK DIVISION

PROBATE COURT

No. _98D-7579_

_____ Elizabeth Beauchamp _____, Plaintiff(s)

v.

_____ Edward Beauchamp _____, Defendant(s)

NOTICE OF APPEARANCE

'O THE REGISTER OF THE ABOVE NAMED COURT:

Please enter my appearance as attorney for ____defendant Edward Beauchamp____

the above entitled case.

ted: ___February 19___, 19_98_

H. A. Lincoln, Jr.
Attorney for ~~Plaintiff~~ H. A. Lincoln, Jr., Esq.
Defendant

Address: ___575 Moody Street___

___Waltham MA 02154___

Tel. No. ___(781) 899-7548___

B.B.O.   #235236

COMMONWEALTH OF MASSACHUSETTS

Norfolk Division

Probate and Family Court

No. 98D-7579

ELIZABETH BEAUCHAMP, Plaintiff

v.

EDWARD BEAUCHAMP, Defendant

DEFENDANT'S ANSWER AND COUNTERCLAIM

Defendant makes the following Answer to Plaintiff's January 21, 1998 Complaint for Divorce.

(1) Defendant admits the allegations in paragraphs 1 to 4.

(2) Defendant denies the allegations in paragraph 5.

(3) Defendant states further that he has never in any way abused the Plaintiff.

COUNTERCLAIM

(1) Defendant states that on January 2, 1998 and on divers other occasions the Plaintiff committed acts of cruel and abusive treatment toward him.

(2) Defendant states further that since January 2, 1998 that there has been an irretrievable breakdown of the marriage.

Wherefore, Defendant requests that he be granted a divorce on the ground of cruel and abusive treatment and on the ground of irretrievable breakdown of the marriage and that the Court grant also the following relief:

(1) custody of the three minor children, Catherine born October 15, 1983 Margaret born January 25, 1985 and George born May 12, 1988.

(2) child support pursuant to the guidelines,

(3) conveyance of the real estate at 39 Elm Street, Dedham, Massachusetts, owned jointly by the parties as tenants by the entirety, as recorded with Norfolk Registry of Deeds at Book 21798, Page 434,

(4) equal division of all other marital assets, and

(5) such other and further relief as shall seem just.

EDWARD BEAUCHAMP
By His Attorney

H. A. Lincoln, Jr.

H. A. Lincoln, Jr., Esq.
575 Moody Street
Waltham MA   02154
(781) 899-7548

February 19, 1998

B.B.O. #235236

CERTIFICATE OF SERVICE

I, H. A. Lincoln, Jr., Esq. hereby certify that I have served this Answer and Counterclaim on Plaintiff Elizabeth Beauchamp by mailing a copy to her first class mail postage prepaid at her residence, 39 Elm Street, Dedham MA 02026 on February 19, 1998.

Signed under pains and penalties of perjury this 19th day of February, 1998.

H. A. Lincoln, Jr.

H. A. Lincoln, Jr., Esq.

Commonwealth of Massachusetts
The Trial Court
__Norfolk___ **Division** **Probate and Family Court Department**   **Docket No.** 98D-7579

Financial Statement
(LONG FORM)

_____Elizabeth Beauchamp_____   V.   _____Edward Beauchamp_____
Plaintiff/Petitioner   Defendant/Petitioner

INSTRUCTIONS: This financial statement should be completed if your income equals or exceeds $75,000.00 or if ordered by the court. All items on both sides of this form must be addressed either with the appropriate amount or the word "none" inserted for items that are not applicable to your personal situation. Additional sheets may be attached to supplement any item. You must complete and attach Schedule A if you are self-employed or have other business income, and/or Schedule B if you own rental property.

I. PERSONAL INFORMATION

Your Name _____Edward Beauchamp_____   Social Security Number _023-43-2280._

Address __28 Old Road__   Franklin   MA   02038
(street address)   (city or town)   (state)   (zip code)

Telephone Number (_508_) _528-4081_ _____ Date of Birth __5-19-57__   Age __41__

Occupation _____Engineer_____

Employer __Raytheon Corp.__   Employer's Telephone Number (_781_)642-4000

Employer's Address __20 Seyon Street__   Waltham   MA   02154
(street address)   (city or town)   (state)   (zip code)

Do you have health insurance coverage [X] Yes [ ] No If **yes**, name of health insurance provider _Harvard Pilgrim_

Do you have any natural, adopted, stepchild(ren), foster child(ren) or children of partners who are living in your household half time or more?

[ ] Yes [X] No   If so, how many child(ren)? _____

II. GROSS WEEKLY INCOME/ RECEIPTS FROM ALL SOURCES (strike inapplicable words)

a)	Base pay, salary, wages	1,721.00
b)	Overtime	--
c)	Part-time job	--
d)	Self-employment (**attach a completed Schedule A**)	--
e)	Tips	--
f)	Commissions- Bonuses	--
g)	Dividends - interest	77.00
h)	Income from trusts and annuities	--
i)	Pension and retirement funds	--
J)	Social Security	--
k)	Disability, unemployment or worker's compensation	--
l)	Public Assistance	--
m)	Child Support - Alimony (actually received)	--
n)	Rental income (**attach completed Schedule B**)	--
o)	Royalties and other rights	--
p)	Contributions from household member(s)	--
q)	Other (specify)	
	110	

TOTAL GROSS WEEKLY INCOME/RECEIPTS (Add items a-q)   _1,798.00_

III. WEEKLY DEDUCTIONS FROM GROSS INCOME

TAX WITHHOLDING

a) Federal tax withholding/estimated payments 430.25
   Number of withholding allowances claimed _____4_____
b) State tax withholding/estimated payments 96.27
   Number of withholding allowances claimed _____4_____

OTHER DEDUCTIONS

c)	F.I.C.A.	
d)	Medicare	82.74
e)	Medical Insurance	50.00
f)	Union Dues	--
g)	Child Support	600.00
h)	Spousal Support	--
i)	Retirement	65.00
j)	Savings	--
k)	Deferred Compensation	--
l)	Credit Union (Loan)	--
m)	Credit Union (Savings)	--
n)	Charitable Contributions	10.00
o)	Life Insurance	22.00
p)	Other (specify) _____	--
q)	Other (specify) _____	--
r)	Other (specify) _____	--

TOTAL WEEKLY DEDUCTIONS FROM PAY (Add items a-r) 1,356.26

IV.   NET WEEKLY INCOME

a) Enter total gross weekly income/receipts 1,798.00
b) Enter total weekly deductions from pay 1,356.26

NET WEEKLY INCOME (Subtract IV(b) from IV(a)) 441.74

V.   GROSS INCOME FROM PRIOR YEAR 85,017.00

(attach copy of all W-2 and 1099 forms for prior year and Schedule A, if self employed)

Number of years you have paid into Social Security _____19_____

VI.   COUNSEL FEES

Retainer amount(s) paid to your attorney(s) 10,000.00
Legal fees incurred, to date, against the retainer(s) 8,000.00
Anticipated range of total legal expense to prosecute this action .... 10,000. to 30,000.

111

VII. WEEKLY EXPENSES NOT DEDUCTED FROM PAY

INSTRUCTIONS: All expense figures must be listed by their WEEKLY total. DO NOT list expenses by their MONTHLY total. In order to compute the weekly expense, divide the monthly expense by 4.3. For example, if your rent is $500.00 per month, divide 500 by 4.3. This will give you a weekly expense of $116.28. Do not duplicate weekly expenses. Strike inapplicable words.

Rent	145.
Mortgage (P & I, Taxes/Insurance, if escrowed)	--
Property taxes and assessments	--
Homeowner's Insurance	--
Tenant's Insurance	--
Maintenance Fees - Condominium Fees	--
Maintenance/Repairs	--
Heat (type:_____)	20.
Electricity	--
Propane/Natural Gas	10.
Telephone	--
Water/Sewer	100.
Food	--
House Supplies	10.
Laundry	15.
Dry cleaning	20.
Clothing	10.
Life insurance	--
Medical insurance	--
Uninsured medical - dental expenses	15.
Incidentals/toiletries	--
Motor vehicle expenses	30.
Fuel	10.
Insurance	20.
Maintenance	--
Loan payment(s)	20.
Entertainment	20.
Vacation	10.
Cable TV	--
Child Support (attach a copy of the order, if issued by a different court)	--
Child(ren)'s Day Care Expense	--
Child(ren)'s Education	--
Education (self)	--
Employment related expenses (which are not reimbursed)	--
Uniforms	--
Travel	--
Required continuing education	--
Other (specify)_____	5.
Lottery tickets	10.
Charitable contributions/Church giving	--
Child(ren)'s allowance	50.
Extraordinary travel expenses for visitation with child(ren)	--
Other (specify) _____	--
Other (specify)_____	--
Other (specify)_____	

TOTAL WEEKLY EXPENSES NOT DEDUCTED FROM PAY 520.

112

VIII. **ASSETS**

INSTRUCTIONS: List all assets including, but not limited to the following. If additional space is needed for any answer or to disclose additional assets an attached sheet may be filed.

A. **REAL ESTATE**

Real Estate — Primary Residence

Address ___39 Elm Street_____ Dedham_____ MA_____
          (street address)   (city or town)   (state)

Title held___Edward and Elizabeth Beauchamp, by the entirety_____

Outstanding 1st mortgage	148,985
Outstanding 2nd mortgage or home equity loan	--
Equity	200,000
Purchase Price of the Property	195,000
Year of Purchase	1983
Current Assessed Value of the Property	298,900
Date of Last Assessment	1997
Fair Market Value of the Property	350,000

Real Estate — Vacation or Second Home (including interest in time share)

Address _____
          (street address)   (city or town)   (state)

Title held	
Outstanding 1st mortgage	
Outstanding 2nd mortgage or home equity loan	
Equity	
Purchase Price of the Property	
Year of Purchase	
Current Assessed Value of the Property	
Date of Last Assessment	
Fair Market Value of the Property	

B. **MOTOR VEHICLES,** including cars, trucks, ATV's, snowmobiles, tractors, motorcycles, boats, recreational vehicles, aircraft, farm machinery, etc.

Type	Minivan
Make	Plymouth
Model	1991 Voyager
Purchase Price of vehicle	$7,100
Year of Purchase	1997
Fair Market Value	$6,500
Outstanding Loan	None
Equity	$6,500 approximately

Type	
Make	
Model	
Purchase Price of vehicle	
Year of Purchase	
Fair Market Value	
Outstanding Loan	
Equity	

113

VIII. ASSETS CONTINUED
C. PENSIONS

	Institution	Account Number	Listed Beneficiary	Current Balance/Value
Defined Benefit Plan	None			
Defined Contribution Plan	Raytheon	03457-Al	Elizabeth Beauchamp	$98,024

D. OTHER ASSETS.
List assets which are held individually, jointly, in the name of another person for your benefit, or held by you for the benefit of your minor child(ren). (List particulars as indicated, e.g., institution/plan name(s) and account number(s), named beneficiaries and current balances, if applicable)

	Institution	Account Number	Listed Beneficiary	Current Balance
Checking Account(s)	Franklin Savings	102243567		$245
Savings Account(s)	Dedham Savings	235790458	Joint with Elizabeth Beauchamp	$15,400
Cash on Hand				$35
Certificate(s) of Deposit	None			--
Credit Union Account(s)	None			--
Funds Held in Escrow	None			--
Stocks	Niagara Falls	AB-1505-2	Joint with Elizabeth Beauchamp	$34.043
Bonds	None			--
Bond Fund(s)	None			--
Notes Held	None			--
Cash in Brokerage Account(s)	None			--
Money Market Account(s)	None			--

	Institution	Account Number	Listed Beneficiary	Current Balance
U.S. Savings Bond(s)	None			--
IRAs	None			--
Keough	None			--
Profit Sharing	None			--
Deferred Compensation	None			--
Other Retirement Plans	None			--
Annuity (please specify whether a tax deferred annuity or a tax sheltered annuity).	None			--
Life Insurance Cash Value (please specify whether a term or a whole/universal life insurance policy).	Bulworth Mutual	$100,000 term 25-63-478	Elizabeth Beauchamp	No Cash Value
Judgments/Liens	None			--
Pending Legacies and/or Inheritances	None			--
Jewelry	None			--
Contents of Safe or Safe Deposit Box	None			--
Firearms	None			--
Collections	Stamps		Approximately	$2,000
Tools/Equipment	None			--
Crops/Livestock	None			--
Home Furnishings (value)			Approximately	$5,000
Art and Antiques	None			--
Other (specify_____)				
Other (specify_____)				

TOTAL ASSETS Approximately | $362,247 |

XI. <u>LIABILITIES</u> (List loans, credit card debt, consumer debt, installment debt, etc. which are not listed elsewhere)

<u>INSTRUCTIONS:</u> **All payment figures must be listed by their WEEKLY amount. DO NOT list payments by their MONTHLY amount. In order to compute the weekly payment, divide the monthly payment by 4.3. For example, if your credit card liability is $500.00 per month, divide 500 by 4.3. This will give you a weekly payment of $116.28.**

CREDITOR	KIND OF DEBT	DATE INCURRED	AMOUNT DUE	WEEKLY PAYMENT
VISA Plus	Credit Card	1997	$4,500	$50
Minus Mastercard	Credit Card	1998	3,500	40
TOTALS			$8,000	$90

CERTIFICATION BY AFFIANT

I certify under the penalties of perjury that the information stated on this Financial Statement and the attached Schedules, if any, is complete, true, and accurate. **I UNDERSTAND THAT WILLFUL MISREPRESENTATION OF ANY OF THE INFORMATION PROVIDED WILL SUBJECT ME TO SANCTIONS AND MAY RESULT IN CRIMINAL CHARGES BEING FILED AGAINST ME.**

March 3, 1998
Date

Edward Beauchamp
Signature

COMMONWEALTH OF MASSACHUSETTS

County of ___Norfolk___

Then personally appeared the above_____Edward Beauchamp_____and declared the

foregoing to be true and correct, before me this___3rd___ day of_____March_____, 199 8 .

H. A. Lincoln, Jr.
Notary Public

My Commission Expires:____12-26-2004____

INSTRUCTIONS: In any case where an attorney is appearing for a party, said attorney MUST complete the Statement by Attorney.

STATEMENT BY ATTORNEY

I, the undersigned attorney, am admitted to practice law in the Commonwealth of Massachusetts — am admitted pro hoc vice for the purposes of this case — and am an officer of the court. As the attorney for the party on whose behalf this Financial Statement is submitted, I hereby state to the court that I have no knowledge that any of the information contained herein is false.

March 3, 1998
Date

H.A. Lincoln, Jr.
Signature

Name of Attorney __H. A. Lincoln, Jr., Esq.__
Please Print

Address _____575 Moody Street, Waltham MA 02154_____

Tel. No. (781) ___899-7548___

BBO # ___235236___

117

INCOME ASSIGNMENT WORKSHEET

NORFOLK DIVISION

PROBATE AND FAMILY COURT

NO. __98D-7579__

PLAINTIFF:

Name __Elizabeth Beauchamp__

Address __39 Elm Street__

__Dedham MA   02026__

Telephone Number __(781) 326-2711__

Social Security No. __083-84-6647__

DEFENDANT:

Name __Edward Beauchamp__

Address __28 Old Road__

__Franklin MA   02038__

Telephone Number __(508) 528-4081__

Social Security No. __023-43-2280__

Obligor's Place of Employment

Employer's Name __Raytheon Corp.__

Address: __20 Seyon Street__

__Waltham MA   02154__

Telephone Number __(781) 642-4000__

Effective Immediately ☒

Suspended ☐

__March 4, 1998__
Date

Obligor to pay $ __600__ per week / ~~month~~

as ~~alimony and /~~ or child support.

Arrearage	$ __--__
Current Order	$ __600__
Arrears Order	$ __--__

Payment made payable to: ☐ DEPARTMENT OF REVENUE

☒ Spouse directly

Send to (to reimburse): ☒ Spouse

☐ DPW-_____ office

☐ Other_____

118

Health Insurance:
Obligor's Insurer __Harvard Pilgrim__   Policy No. __13-14-04B__

Commonwealth of Massachusetts

THE TRIAL COURT
THE PROBATE AND FAMILY COURT DEPARTMENT

__Norfolk__ Division   Docket No. __98D-7579__

REQUEST FOR ~~TRIAL~~ — PRE-TRIAL ASSIGNMENT
THIS FORM SHOULD **NOT** BE USED FOR MARK-UP OF TEMPORARY ORDERS AND MOTIONS
Please print or type

Please assign
for hearing: __Elizabeth Beauchamp__

                                                              Plaintiff

                              v.

                 __Edward Beauchamp__

                                                              Defendant

TYPE OF CASE __Divorce__   TIME REQUIRED __3 hours__   HEARING AT __Dedham__

( ) Uncontested

(x) Contested

   ( ) Merits
   ( ) Custody
   (X) Support
   (X) Visitation
   (X) 208, § 34 Division of Property
   ( ) Other _____

The following papers must be on file before
cases can be assigned for hearing:

(X) Summons or Return of Service
(X) Marriage Certificate
(X) Statistical Form R408
(X) Financial Statement (Supp. Rule 401)
( ) Affidavits of Both Parties (1A Divorces)
( ) Notarized Agreement (1A Divorces)
( ) _____

Has Discovery Been Completed   (X) Yes   ( ) No

Has This Case Been Pre-Tried   ( ) Yes   (X) No

I hereby certify that, in my opinion, this case is ready for trial.

Requested by: Opposing Counsel:

__Elizabeth Beauchamp__   Name   __H. A. Lincoln, Jr., Esq.__

__39 Elm Street, Dedham MA 02026__   Address   __575 Moody St. Waltham MA 02154__
                                     and
__(781) 326-2711__   Phone No. __(781) 899-7548__

- -

FOR REGISTER'S USE ONLY
ACTION

The above-entitled matter has been assigned for

_____ (Trial) _____ (Pre-Trial Conference)

at _____ on _____ 19____, at _____

_____ . Returned without action. Data Incomplete. See above.

119

Clerk's Initials

Register of Probate
/82

COMMONWEALTH OF MASSACHUSETTS
THE TRIAL COURT
THE PROBATE AND FAMILY COURT DEPARTMENT

NORFOLK DIVISION

DOCKET NO. 98D-7579

Elizabeth Beauchamp _____ , Plaintiff

v.

Edward Beauchamp _____ , Defendant

PRE-TRIAL NOTICE AND ORDER

The above-entitled action is set for a pre-trial conference before a Justice of the Probate and Family Court on _____ June 1, 1998 _____ at Dedham, MA at _____ 9:00 am. _____ .

Prior to pre-trial conference counsel and parties shall meet and shall confer in person with each other. Each counsel must exchange with each other prior to the conference and file with the court at the time of pre-trial a memorandum setting forth:

A. A comprehensive written stipulation of all uncontested facts.

B. A statement of contested issues of fact and law and progress of agreement on such, if any.

C. Certification that all discovery has been completed; if discovery has not been completed, list what remains to be done.

D. Copies of current financial statements and any other pertinent financial data.

E. A list of potential witnesses.

F. A list of all exhibits which counsel intend to introduce at the trial.

G. Depositions proposed to be used as evidence to be read into the record. Use of depositions at the trial are subject to provisions of Mass. R. Dom. Rel. P. 32.

H. Stipulation of current value(s), and cost of all realty and personalty in issue. In the event the parties are unable to agree as to current values, counsel and parties are to submit an opinion of fair market value, either themselves or by an appraiser.

I. A realistic time estimate of trial time.

J. If there are issues of alimony and the assignment of property under Chapter 208, section 34 a written offer of proof setting forth the evidence each party intends to produce with respect to each of the factors enumerated under the statute should be filed.

If any party objects to the admissibility of any of the above listed matters, the name of the party objecting and the grounds for objection shall be set forth.

The case may be ordered to immediate trial on the date of the pre-trial if the court determines at the pre-trial that (a) the parties to the action will be the only witnesses; or (b) one party, through a failure to appear at the pre-trial or otherwise, will not present a case; or (c) such commencement of trial is necessary in the judge's discretion to accomplish justice.

IH - 52 50

(Over)

PRE-TRIAL NOTICE AND ORDER

At such pre-trial conference, the Court will consider the simplification of the issues, the necessity of amendments to the pleadings, the prospects of settlement, or such other matters as may aid in the trial or any other disposition of the action.

At the conclusion of such pre-trial conference, an appropriate order will be entered reflecting the action taken at such conference.

All trial counsel and parties shall attend the pre-trial conference. Failure of counsel to appear at any scheduled pre-trial conference or otherwise to comply with the provisions of this order will result in the imposition of such sanctions as the Court may deem appropriate.

If settlement is achieved prior to or at the pre-trial conference, the pre-trial conference time may be utilized for a hearing on an uncontested basis.

Dated this _____3 rd_____ day of _____April_____ , 19 _98_

_____David H. Kopelman_____

Justice, Probate and Family Court

NOTE: All inquiries must be directed ONLY to: Ed Harrington

121

COMMONWEALTH OF MASSACHUSETTS

Norfolk County

Probate and Family Court
No. 98D-7579

ELIZABETH BEAUCHAMP, Plaintiff

v.

PRE-TRIAL MEMORANDUM

EDWARD BEAUCHAMP, Defendant

OF ELIZABETH BEAUCHAMP

A.   UNCONTESTED FACTS

We were married at Walpole, Massachusetts on July 1, 1981 and have three
children, Catherine, born October 15, 1987, Margaret, born January 25, 1989,
and George, born May 12, 1992. The children live with me in the marital home
at 39 Elm Street, Dedham. We have been separated since January 21, 1998, when
I obtained emergency vacate, restraining and custody orders from this court.

Mr. Beauchamp is employed by Raytheon in Waltham as an engineer. His
March 3, 1998 financial statement indicates his gross income is $89,500 per
year ($1,721 per week). I am unemployed and have not worked full time since
the marriage, at Mr. Beauchamp's request. I have been the primary caretaker
of the three children.

We own jointly the marital home at 39 Elm Street, Dedham. The real estate
has a fair market value of $350,000 and an outstanding mortgage of approximately
$150,000. There is about $50,000 in savings and stocks, on which there is a
temporary restraining order, as well as a $98,000 pension.

B.   CONTESTED ISSUES OF FACT

At issue are the amount and duration of child support and alimony payments;
the amount and duration of life insurance; payment of uninsured medical costs;
division of personal property; division of savings, stocks and pension; and
disposition of the marital real estate.

Mr. Beauchamp requested custody in his February 19, 1998 Answer and
Counterclaim, but he has never moved for the appointment of guardian ad litem
or an investigation by a family service officer, nor otherwise shown any intent
to litigate the issue of custody.

I have met on two occasions with my husband and his attorney in an effort
to reach agreement, but have been unable to do so.

122

C.   DISCOVERY

Discovery has been completed.

D.   FINANCIAL STATEMENTS

Current financial statements are on file with the court.

E.   POTENTIAL WITNESSES

Elizabeth Beauchamp, Plaintiff

Edward Beauchamp, Defendant

I reserve the right to call additional witnesses as needed to rebut testimony offered by Defendant or his witnesses.

F.   EXHIBITS

Defendant's payroll and benefits records.

Appraisal of the marital home at 39 Elm Street, Dedham. I reserve the right to introduce other exhibits needed for rebuttal.

G.   DEPOSITIONS

There are none.

H.   CURRENT VALUES OF REALTY

We have stipulated that the marital home in Dedham has a fair market value of $350,000 and that the outstanding mortgage balance is approximately $150,000.

I.   TRIAL TIME

It is estimated that 5 hours of trial time will be required.

J.   CHAPTER 208, SECTION 34 FACTORS

<u>Length of marriage</u> We have been married for almost 17 years.

<u>Age of the parties</u> I am 38 years old. Mr. Beauchamp is 41.

<u>Health</u> I have acute fibromyalgia. Mr. Beauchamp is in good health.

<u>Occupation</u> I have not worked since the marriage. Mr. Beauchamp works as an engineer at Raytheon in Waltham. He has been there 19 years.

<u>Vocational skills and employability</u> I have no vocational skills, and am unemployable because of poor health and the demands of raising our three

children. When we got married, Mr. Beauchamp asked me to quit my job as a waitress and become a full-time homemaker, and I agreed to do that. Mr. Beauchamp has been employed as an engineer for the past 19 years and has job security in the field for which he was trained.

Needs and liabilities Each of us requires income for individual living expenses, and I need continuing child support for the children.

Amount and sources of income Mr. Beauchamp earns $1,721 per week, and he pays $600 weekly as child support. I have no other source of income.

Amount of property We own jointly the marital home in Dedham which has about $200,000 in equity. We have savings of $15,400, stocks worth about $35,000, and Mr. Beauchamp's pension is worth about $98,000.

Contribution of each to the property Both of us contributed to the acquisition and preservation of our property, all of which was acquired during the marriage. While Mr. Beauchamp worked at Raytheon and traveled extensively, I took care of our three children and our home, managed all the finances, did all of the shopping, cooking and cleaning and entertained his business associates on a regular basis. My parents gave us the downpayment on the house.

Opportunity for future acquisition of property and income Mr. Beauchamp's income of $89,500 per year clearly indicates that he has the ability to acquire property hereafter. He receives annual raises of approximately 5% along with numerous benefits. He also expects a large inheritance from his parents.

Because of my lack of vocational skills, absence from the job market and poor health, I have no prospect of earning any income in the future, and no prospect of acquiring additional property. Also my parents are now deceased.

Homemaking contribution I have made the entire contribution as homemaker for the family and was the primary caretaker of the children.

Conduct of the parties during the marriage I sought to preserve the marriage. My husband did not. He was abusive to me and when he left I found out that for years he had been seeing another woman with whom he now lives.

Present and future needs of the dependent children Catherine is 10, Margaret is 9 and George is 6 years old. The children have all the usual expenses: food, clothing, shelter, learning, etc. They are all great learners and good students, and my main concern regarding their future needs is that they get a good education, including four years of college.

June 1, 1998

Respectfully submitted,

Elizabeth Beauchamp

124

Commonwealth of Massachusetts

11797

PROBATE AND FAMILY COURT DEPARTMENT
CASSETTE COPY REQUEST FORM

Instructions: Person requesting cassette shall complete items 1 - 9 and 12. Registry personnel processing request will complete items 10, 11, 13 - 19. Part II will be completed at Duplicating Center.

Use a separate form for each case. Registry will keep the pink copy and send the white and yellow copies with the original cassette to the duplicating center. The white (original) copy will be returned to the originating registry with the cassette and should be placed with the case papers.

PART I

(1) .... Norfolk .... Division (2) Case name Elizabeth Beauchamp v. Edward .... (3) Case No. 98D-7579

Beauchamp

Person(s) Requesting Copies

(4) H. A. Lincoln, Jr., Esq.
(name)
575 Moody Street
(address)
Waltham MA 02154

(5) Telephone No. (781) 899-7548

(6) (check one)   ☒ Attorney ☐
☐ Judge   ☐ Party   ☐
☐ Other (specify ....)

(7) If (6) is "other", has the trial judge approved this request per Rule 201?
☐ Y   ☐ N   ☐ N/A

(8) Number of copies of the record which this person wants ☒ 1 ☐ 2 ☐ ____

(9) Costs waived for indigent under G.L. c. 261?   ☐ Y   ☐ N   ☐ N/A

(10) Serial Nos. ....

(11) Cost: (including postage) ....

(4) ....
(name)
....
(address)
....

(5) Telephone No. ....

(6) (check one)   ☐ Attorney ☐
☐ Judge   ☐ Party   ☐
☐ Other (specify: ....)

(7) If (6) is "other", has the trial judge approved this request per Rule 201?
☐ Y   ☐ N   ☐ N/A

(8) Number of copies of the record which this person wants ☐ 1 ☐ 2 ☐ ____

(9) Costs waived for indigent under G.L. c. 261?   ☐ Y   ☐ N   ☐ N/A

(10) Serial Nos. ....

(11) Cost: (including postage) ....

(4) ....
(name)
....
(address)
....

(5) Telephone No. ....

(6) (check one)   ☐ Attorney ☐
☐ Judge   ☐ Party   ☐
☐ Other (specify: ....)

(7) If (6) is "other", has the trial judge approved this request per Rule 201?
☐ Y   ☐ N   ☐ N/A

(8) Number of copies of the record which this person wants ☐ 1 ☐ 2 ☐ ____

(9) Costs waived for indigent under G.L. c. 261?   ☐ Y   ☐ N   ☐ N/A

(10) Serial Nos. ....

(11) Cost: (including postage) ....

Recording to be Copied

(12) Nature of the proceeding: ☐ Civil Trial ☒ Divorce ☐ Other civil proceeding (specify.........................)
☐ Probate Trial ☐ Contempt hearing ☐ Other Divorce proceeding (specify.........................)
☐ Equity   ☐ Adoption   ☐ Abuse Prev.   ☐ Motion   ☐ Guardianship   ☐ TRO

(13) Tape No.	Beginning (14) Index No.	Ending (15) Index No.	Judge (16) Presiding	Date (17) Recorded	(18) Special instructions/comments
			Kopelman	10-1-98	Divorce Trial 9am – 1 pm
					and 2pm – 4 pm

(19) Has the person initiating this request represented that he has notified all parties of his intention to make this request, as required by Rule 201   ☒ Y   ☐ N   ☐ N/A

H. A. Lincoln Jr.
(signature of person placing order)

....
(signature and title of court employee taking this order)

Date 10-2-98

PART II
(TO BE COMPLETED BY DUPLICATING OFFICE)

Returned herewith, original tapes numbered ....
and cassette copies bearing the above noted serial number(s).

....   **Duplicating Office**   Date ....

125

COMMONWEALTH OF MASSACHUSETTS

Norfolk _____ SS.

PROBATE COURT
NO. 98D-7579-

Elizabeth Beauchamp _____ PLAINTIFF

vs

NOTICE OF APPEAL

Edward Beauchamp _____ DEFENDANT

Notice is hereby given that ____ Edward Beauchamp ____
(Appellant)
the above-named ~~plaintiff~~ - defendant - a party in the above-
named matter hereby appeals to the Appeals Court (from the Order
(describing it))

from the custody, child support, alimony and property distribution

provisions of the Divorce Judgment Nisi

entered in this action on November 5, 1998. _____ .
(Date)

November 9, 1998

SIGNED _____ H. A. Lincoln, Jr. _____

Atty. for Appellant H. A. Lincoln, Jr., Esc

Address 575 Moody Street, Waltham MA 02154

Telephone Number (781) 899-7548

B.B.O. #235236

126

Commonwealth of Massachusetts
The Trial Court

Middlesex **Division**   **Probate and Family Court Department**   Docket No. 95D-2149

☒ **Civil**

Complaint for   **Contempt**

☐ **Criminal**

_____ Helen Zukofski _____, Plaintiff

v.

_____ David Zukofski _____, Defendant

1) Plaintiff, who resides at _77 Maple Road, Malden, Middlesex County, Massachusetts_

   was - is - the spouse of defendant, who now resides at _656 North Street, Taunton,_

   Bristol County, Massachusetts

2) By judgment - order - of the Court, dated_ September 13, 1995 _,defendant was ordered:

   ☒ to pay alimony - support of minor children - in the sum of $ _275_
   forthwith and the further sum of $ _275_ weekly - monthly - thereafter
   ☐ to grant plaintiff visitation rights with _____

   _____

   ☐ not to impose any restraint on the personal liberty of plaintiff
   ☐ to pay health insurance premiums for the plaintiff and/or minor child(ren)
   ☒ to pay reasonable medical and dental expenses
   ☐ _____

   and said judgment - order - is still in force.

3) Defendant has not obeyed that judgment - order - and
   ☒ is in arrears of court-ordered support payments
   ☒ there now remains due and unpaid to plaintiff the sum of $ _1,375_
   plus such further amounts as may accrue to the date of hearing
   ☐ plaintiff has been denied visitation rights on _____

   ☒ has violated the order on _June 2, 1998_
   _____ by_____
   refusing since then to pay child support, or to reimburse me for
   dental bills of the children, in the amount of $150.

   _____

) Wherefore, plaintiff requests that defendant be required to appear before this Court to show cause why said defendant should not be adjudged in contempt of Court and for such other relief as to said Court may seem just.

Date _July 8, 1998_   Name_____

_____ Helen Zukofski _____
                    PRINT NAME

127   Address_ 77 Maple Road _

_____ Malden MA   02148 _

Tel. No. (617) _322-7500_

Commonwealth of Massachusetts
The Trial Court
_____Middlesex_____ **Division**   **Probate and Family Court Department**   **Docket No.** 95D-2149

Contempt Summons

_____Helen Zukofski_____ , Plaintiff

v.

_____David Zukofski_____ , Defendant

To the above named Defendant:

You are ordered to appear at a Probate and Family Court to be held at __Cambridge_____

in said County of __Middlesex_____ on _August 14_, 19 _98_,
at ten o'clock in the forenoon to show cause why you should not be held in civil and/or criminal contempt, the penalty for which may be a jail sentence.

You are hereby summoned and required to serve upon _____Helen Zukofski_____

_____ plaintiff's ~~attorney~~ whose address is __77 Maple Road__

_Malden MA 02148_____
your answer, if any, to the complaint which is herewith served upon you, within 7 days after service of this summons upon you, exclusive of the day of service. You are also required to file your answer, if any, to the complaint in the office of the Register of this Court at __Cambridge_____
either before service upon plaintiff's attorney or within a reasonable time thereafter.

Failure to appear on this date may result in the issuance of an order for your arrest.

Witness __Sheila E. McGovern_____ , Esquire, First Justice of said

Court at __Cambridge_____

this _____14th_____ day of _____July_____ , 19 _98_____ .

Marie A. Gardin
Acting Register

Register of Probate

128

CJ-D 113 (1/89)

Commonwealth of Massachusetts
The Trial Court
Probate and Family Court Department

Docket No. 95D-2149

Contempt Summons

Helen Zukofski , Plaintiff

v.

David Zukofski , Defendant

Return Of Service

I certify under the penalties of perjury that on ___July 17___ , 19_98_ , I served a co₁y of the within summons, together with a copy of the complaint in this action, upon the within named defendant by:

leaving a copy taped to the door of defendant's residence at 656 North Street, Taunton MA while also sending additional copies to defendant by first class mail.

Date _July 17, 1998_

Signature _John Mudgett_

129   John Mudgett Constable

DOCKET NO.

TRIAL COURT OF MASSACHUSETTS

BOSTON MUNICIPAL COURT	X DISTRICT COURT	PROBATE & FAMILY COURT	SUPERIOR COURT	Framingham DIVISION

A

B Name of Plaintiff (person seeking protection)
Laura Gardner

Name of Defendant (person accused of abuse)
Thomas Gardner

Plaintiff's Address. DO NOT complete if the Plaintiff is asking the Court to keep it confidential. *See K. 4. below.*

Def. Date of Birth	Defendant's Alias, if any
11-11-54	

C

32 Concord Road
Sudbury MA 01776

Defendant's Address

32 Concord Road
Sudbury MA 01776

Day Phone (978)
443-2515

G

Daytime Phone No. (978) 443-1776

Sex: X M ☐ F

If the Plaintiff left a former residence to avoid abuse, write that address here:

Social Security # 071-41-2957	Place of Birth Sudbury MA

E

I ᵡ am over the age of eighteen.

I ☐ am under the age of eighteen, and _____,

my _____(relationship to Plaintiff) has filed this complaint for me.

Defendant's Mother's Maiden Name (first & last)
Marian Messina

Defendant's Father's Name (first & last)
Robert Gardner

F

The Defendant ☐ is ᵡ is not under the age of eighteen.

To my knowledge, the Defendant possesses the following guns, ammunition, firearms identification card, and/or license to carry:

H The Defendant and Plaintiff:

X are currently married to each other

☐ were formerly married to each other

☐ are not married but we are related to each other by blood or marriage; specifically, the Defendant is my _____

Are there any prior or pending court actions in any state or country involving the Plaintiff and the Defendant for divorce, annulment, separate support, legal separation or abuse prevention? X No ☐ Yes
If Yes, give Court, type of case, date, and (if available) docket no.

X are the parents of one or more children

☐ are not related but live in the same household

☐ were formerly members of the same household

☐ are or were in a dating or engagement relationship.

I Does the Plaintiff have any children? ☐ No X Yes If yes, the Plaintiff shall complete the appropriate parts of Page 2.

J On or about (dates) March 5, 1998 _____ I suffered abuse when the Defendant:

☐ attempted to cause me physical harm   ☒ placed me in fear of imminent serious physical harm

X caused me physical harm   ☐ caused me to engage in sexual relations by force, threat of force or duress

THEREFORE, I ASK THE COURT TO ORDER:

X 1. the Defendant to stop abusing me by harming, threatening or attempting to harm me physically, or placing me in fear of imminent serious physical harm, or by using force, threat or duress to make me engage in sexual relations unwillingly.

X 2. the Defendant not to contact me, unless authorized to do so by the Court.

X 3. the Defendant to leave and remain away from my residence which is located at:
32 Concord Road, Sudbury MA 01776
If this is an apartment building or other multiple family dwelling, check here ☐

☐ 4. that my address be impounded to prevent its disclosure to the Defendant, the Defendant's attorney, or the public.
Attach Request for Address Impoundment form to this Complaint.

X 5. the Defendant to leave and remain away from my workplace which is located at:
The Wayside Inn, 72 Wayside Inn Road, Sudbury MA 01776

☐ 6. the Defendant to pay me $_____ in compensation for the following losses suffered as a direct result of the abuse:

You may not obtain an Order from the Boston Municipal Court or a District or Superior Court covering the following item 7 if there is a prior or pending Order for support from the Probate and Family Court.

X 7. the Defendant, who has a legal obligation to do so, to pay temporary support for me.

X 8. the relief requested on page two of this Complaint pertaining to my minor child or children.

☐ 9. the following: _____

X 10. the relief I have requested, except for temporary support for me and/or my child(ren) and for compensation for losses suffered, without advance notice to the Defendant because there is a substantial likelihood of immediate danger of abuse. I understand that if the Court issues such a temporary Order, the Court will schedule a hearing within 10 court business days to determine whether such a temporary Order should be continued, and I must appear in Court on that day if I wish the Order to be continued.

DATE	PLAINTIFF'S SIGNATURE		Please complete affidavit on reverse of this page
3-5-98	X *Laura Gardner* 130		

This is a request for a civil order to protect the Plaintiff from future abuse. The actions of the Defendant may also constitute a crime subject to criminal penalties. For information about filing a criminal complaint, you can talk with the District Attorney's Office for the location where the alleged abuse occurred.

<table>
<tr><td>

COMPLAINT FOR PROTECTION
FROM ABUSE
(G.L. c.209A) Page 2 of 2
</td><td>

COURT USE ONLY – DOCKET NO.
</td><td>

TRIAL COURT OF MASSACHUSETTS
</td></tr>
</table>

ISSUES PERTAINING TO CHILDREN

A. **RELATED PROCEEDINGS.** Is there any proceeding that the Plaintiff knows of or has participated in which is pending or has been concluded in any Court in the Commonwealth or any other state or country involving the care or custody of the child or children of the parties? ☐ YES ☒ NO
If Yes, the Plaintiff shall complete and file with this Complaint an Affidavit Disclosing Care or Custody Proceedings as required by Trial Court Uniform Rule IV, and provide copies of documents required by the Rule. This Affidavit and related information are available from the office of the Clerk-Magistrate or Register of Probate of the Court.

B. **RELATED PROCEEDINGS.** Are there any prior or pending court actions in any state or country involving the Plaintiff and the Defendant for paternity: ☐ YES ☒ NO

C. **CUSTODY.**
The Plaintiff may not obtain an Order from the Boston Municipal Court or a District or Superior Court for custody if there is a prior or pending Order for custody from the Probate and Family Court or Juvenile Court.
☒ I request custody of the following minor child or children of the parties:

NAME	DATE OF BIRTH	NAME	DATE OF BIRTH
Charlotte	3-13-90		
Lucille	3-23-95		

D. **CONTACT WITH CHILDREN.** I ask the Court to order the Defendant not to contact the following child or children unless authorized to do so by the Court:

NAME	NAME
Charlotte Gardner	
Lucille Gardner	

The specific reasons for this request are: <u>My husband has been abusive to me in front of the</u> <u>children and they are extremely fearful of him. I feel we will all need counseling</u> <u>now and that future visits should be supervised.</u>

If the Plaintiff alleges that the Defendant has abused the above-named child or children, a separate Complaint may be filed on behalf of each child.

E. **VISITATION.** If the Plaintiff is filing this Complaint in the Probate and Family Court, the Plaintiff may request a Visitation Order. Such Orders are not available in other Courts. Regarding visitation, I ask the Court to
☐ permit visitation.
☒ order no visitation between the Defendant and our minor child or children.
☐ permit visitation only at the following visitation center:_____
_____to be paid for by _____ (name).
☐ permit only visitation supervised by _____ (name).
at the following times:_____
_____to be paid for by _____ (name).
☐ order visitation only if a third party, _____ (name) , picks up and
drops off our minor child or children.

F. **TEMPORARY SUPPORT.**
The Plaintiff may not obtain an Order from the Boston Municipal Court or a District or Superior Court for temporary support if there is a prior or pending Order for support from the Probate and Family Court or Juvenile Court.

☒ I ask the Court to order the Defendant, who has a legal obligation to do so, to pay temporary support for any children in my custody. 131

DATE	PLAINTIFF'S SIGNATURE
3-5-98	X Laura Gardner

A 1A (9/95)

COURT COPY

AFFIDAVIT	Describe in detail the most recent incidents of abuse. The Judge requires as much information as possible, such as what happened, each person's actions, the dates, locations, any injuries, and any medical or other services sought. Also describe any history of abuse, with as much of the above detail as possible.

On or about __March 5__ , 199 __8__ , the Defendant __came home about 2 a.m. after being out all__ __night. He woke me up from a sound sleep and started yelling obscenities at me, blaming__ __me for his problems at work. I said, "What are you doing, waking me up like this?"__ __He became enraged and started punching me in the face, causing my mouth to bleed.__

I called 911 as soon as I was able to get away from him. He yanked the phone out of the wall as I was talking to the dispatcher. The police arrived 5 minutes later. They arrested my husband and took him away.

The children woke up when they heard me screaming. They saw what their father was doing to me, and then they saw the police come and take him away in handcuffs. They are completely shaken up and traumatized.

This is not the first time my husband has hit me, but he has never been this violent and crazy before. For whatever reason, he has become unable to control his anger, and I am truly afraid of him.

I can't live like this any more and don't want my children to be subjected to any more scenes like this.

If more space is needed, attach additional pages and check this box: ☐

I declare under penalty of perjury that all statements of fact made above, and in any additional pages attached, are true.

DATE SIGNED	PLAINTIFF'S SIGNATURE
3-5-98	x _Laura Gardner_

WITNESSED BY	PRINTED NAME OF WITNESS	TITLE/RANK OF WITNESS
x _Tara Thomas_	Tara Thomas	Probation Officer

INSTRUCTIONS TO THE PLAINTIFF

PROTECTION FROM ABUSE

Under chapter 209A of Massachusetts General Laws, Judges can make Orders to protect people from abuse by family or household members. These Orders will be recorded and enforced by law enforcement agencies. They are commonly called "Abuse Prevention Orders" or "Restraining Orders" or "209A Orders." In an emergency that occurs after court hours or on weekends. you may ask your local police to put you in contact with a Judge.

CHECKLIST OF FORMS

COMPLAINT FORM: To request an Abuse Prevention Order, you must fill out a two-page Complaint form and any other appropriate forms. There is no filing fee. You are the "Plaintiff." The person who you allege has abused you is the "Defendant."

Part D: If either you or the Defendant is under the age of 18, indicate that in Part D. The law provides that such cases are not open to public inspection and are available only to the Plaintiff, the Plaintiff's attorney. the person under 18. or a parent or guardian of the person under 18. If you and the Defendant are both over 18. court records of this matter will generally be open to public inspection. If you have good reasons to ask the Judge to keep other parts of the court record confidential, you may file a written request (a "motion") asking the Judge to do so. Usually, a general preference for privacy is not a sufficient reason to permit court records to be kept confidential.

Part F: If you answer "Yes," please bring with you to the courthouse any legal papers you have from any such court proceeding.

Part K: In number 6, financial losses may include, but are not limited to. lost earnings or support. costs for restoring utilities, replacement costs for locks or personal property removed or destroyed. medical and moving expenses. and reasonable attorneys' fees.

AFFIDAVIT: On the back of the first (white) copy of the Complaint form is an affidavit where you should describe the abuse. When you are requesting relief after court hours, you must fill it out, unless a Judge provides to the contrary.

REQUEST FOR ADDRESS IMPOUNDMENT FORM: If you are asking the Court to keep your address confidential, check number 4 in Part K at the bottom of the Complaint form. Obtain a Request for Address Impoundment form from the office of the Clerk-Magistrate or the Register of Probate, complete it, seal it in an envelope marked "PLAINTIFF'S ADDRESS - CONFIDENTIAL." and staple the envelope to the Court (white) copy of the Complaint form.

AFFIDAVIT DISCLOSING CARE OR CUSTODY PROCEEDINGS: If you have any children, check "Yes" in Part I on page one of the Complaint form, complete the top and any other appropriate parts of page two, and follow instructions in item A on page two for completing an Affidavit Disclosing Care or Custody Proceedings.

DEFENDANT INFORMATION FORM: This form describes the Defendant and where that person can be found. It will help law enforcement officers find that person to deliver the Order.

Commonwealth of Massachusetts
The Trial Court
Probate and Family Court Department

<u>Norfolk</u> **Division**

Docket No. <u>88D-4591</u>

Complaint For Modification

<u>Catherine Norton formerly Holmes</u> , Plaintiff

v.

<u>Kevin Holmes</u> , Defendant

1. Plaintiff, who resides at <u>39 Farm Road</u> <u>Bellingham</u> <u>Norfolk</u>
   (Street and No.) (City or Town) (County)
   <u>Massachusetts</u> <u>02019</u> was/is the spouse of defendant, who resides at
   (State) (Zip)
   <u>445 Main Street</u> <u>Blackstone</u> <u>Norfolk</u> <u>Massachusetts</u> <u>01504</u>
   (Street and No.) (City or Town) (County) (State) (Zip)

*2. This Court, on <u>August 8</u> , 19<u>88</u> , Docket No. <u>88D-4591</u>
   ordered that <u>defendant pay child support in the amount of $250 per week</u>
   <u>for Gary, born 5-16-81, and Anne, born 12-12-85.</u>

3. Since that date, the following changes in the circumstances have occurred:
   <u>My expenses for both children have increased considerably and</u>
   <u>Gary has been accepted at UMass-Amherst.</u>

4. Wherefore, plaintiff requests that the Court order judgment of <u>divorce</u>
   Docket No. <u>88D-4591</u> , be modified by <u>awarding child support</u>
   <u>pursuant to the guidelines and by ordering defendant to contribute to the</u>
   <u>cost of Gary's college education.</u>

Date <u>April 8, 1998</u>

Signature <u>Catherine Norton</u>

Address <u>39 Farm Road, Bellingham MA</u>
<u>02019</u>

Tel. No. <u>(508) 883-8617</u>

*Other modifications must also be set out.

CJ-D104 (8/88)

134

COMMONWEALTH OF MASSACHUSETTS

Norfolk Division

Probate and Family Court

No. 88D-4591

CATHERINE NORTON, Plaintiff

v.

KEVIN HOLMES, Defendant

PLAINTIFF'S MOTION FOR A TEMPORARY ORDER FOR CHILD SUPPORT PURSUANT

TO THE GUIDELINES AND FOR PAYMENT OF 50% OF COLLEGE EXPENSES

Plaintiff CATHERINE NORTON requests that Defendant KEVIN HOLMES be required to pay child support pursuant to the guidelines for the two minor children of the marriage, GARY born 5-16-81 and ANNE born 12-12-85.

Plaintiff requests further that Defendant be ordered to pay 50% of GARY'S college education expenses. GARY has just been accepted at UMass Amherst and would like very much to go and board there.

Respectfully submitted

Catherine Norton
Catherine Norton, Plaintiff

April 10, 1998

Certificate of Service

I, Catherine Norton hereby swear and affirm that I have served a copy of this Motion and attached Proposed Order on Defendant Kevin Holmes by sending a copy to him by first class mail, postage prepaid at his residence 445 Main Street, Blackstone MA 01504 together with notice that a hearing has been scheduled in Dedham on the 17th day of June, 1998 at 9 a.m.

Signed under pains and penalties of perjury.

Catherine Norton
Catherine Norton

135

COMMONWEALTH OF MASSACHUSETTS

Norfolk Division   Probate and Family Court

                                              No.   88D-4591

CATHERINE NORTON, Plaintiff

v.

KEVIN HOLMES, Defendant

PLAINTIFF'S PROPOSED ORDER

The August 8, 1998 Divorce Judgment is hereby modified as follows.

(1) Defendant shall pay child support pursuant to the guidelines in the
     amount of $450 per week for the two minor children, GARY born 5-16-81
     and ANNE born 12-12-85, by wage assignment effective immediately.

(2) Defendant shall pay 50% of the undergraduate college expenses of GARY
     HOLMES at the University of Massachusetts at Amherst.

                                    _____

                                    Justice, Probate and Family Court

_____ 1998

COMMONWEALTH OF MASSACHUSETTS

Norfolk Division

Probate and Family Court
No. 88D-4591

CATHERINE NORTON, Plaintiff

v.

KEVIN HOLMES, Defendant

PLAINTIFF'S MOTION TO COMPEL PRODUCTION OF FINANCIAL STATEMENT AND DOCUMENTS REQUIRED BY RULE 410, MANDATORY SELF-DISCLOSURE AND FOR COSTS

Plaintiff CATHERINE NORTON hereby requests that Defendant KEVIN HOLMES be required to produce a current, signed financial statement, along with copies of all the documents required by Rule 410, including but not limited to federal and state tax returns, W-2s, 1099s and bank statements, securities and pension statements for the last 3 years, four most recent pay stubs and documentation regarding health insurance coverage, on or before June 1, 1998, so that Plaintiff may have a reasonably suficient amount of time to review same prior to the June 12, 1998 hearing on her motion for temporary orders on child support and contribution to college expenses.

Plaintiff states that Defendant was served with the Complaint, Summons and Motion for temporary orders on child support and college education on April 10, 1998; that 45 days elapsed on June 1, 1998; and that Defendant failed to produce a financial statement (pursuant to Rule 401) or the documents required by the Mandatory Self-disclosure provisions of Rule 410 within 45 days of service.

If Defendant fails to produce the financial statement and documents required by Rule 410, Plaintiff requests that he be sanctioned and assessed costs of service ($40), consultation with an attorney ($160) and lost wages of the Plaintiff ($200) for attendance at hearing on this motion on June 4, 1998.

Respectfully submitted

June 2, 1998
For Hearing June 12, 1998

Catherine Norton

Catherine Norton

137

Certificate of Service

I, Catherine Norton hereby swear and affirm that I have served a copy of this motion on Defendant Kevin Holmes by sending a copy to him by first class mail, postage prepaid at his residence 445 Main Street, Blackstone MA 01504 together with notice that a hearing has been scheduled in Dedham on the 12th day of June, 1998 at 9 a.m.

Signed under pains and penalties of perjury this 2nd day of June, 1998.

Catherine Norton

Catherine Norton

COMMONWEALTH OF MASSACHUSETTS

Norfolk Division

Probate and Family Court
No. 88D-4591

CATHERINE NORTON, Plaintiff

v.

KEVIN HOLMES, Defendant

DEFENDANT'S MOTION FOR RECONSIDERATION

I, KEVIN HOLMES, hereby request that the Court reconsider and set aside its Temporary Order of June 17, 1998 for the following reasons:

(1) I am unable to pay the increased child support order of $450 per week to Plaintiff because of the financial obligations which I have to my three children with my present wife Jean Holmes. These children are ages 3, 5 and 8 years old and they are entirely dependent on me for support.

(2) I am responsible for all the expenses of this family, as my wife is at home with the children and is not gainfully employed.

(3) Plaintiff Catherine Norton shares expenses with her husband who is employed as a bank vice president. He drives a Jaguar and is always taking Catherine on expensive vacations, without the children. Gary and Anne go camping with us instead.

(4) For years I have been paying $250 per week to Plaintiff as child support for our two children. They have never wanted for anything.

(5) I do not have the resources to pay 50% of GARY's expenses at UMass. I wish I did but we have no savings and our credit cards are maxed out.

(6) This past week, I applied to three different lending institutions and I was turned down for a loan every time. They all said the same thing, that I don't have the present ability to repay the loan that I would need to contribute to Gary's college expenses.

(7) Gary has told me that he is willing and able to take a work-study job and to apply for loans, but that his mother won't allow it.

(8) My brother and I worked our way through college and I always thought that it was good for us.

(9) I am trying to dig myself out of a hole financially and just do not have the means to comply with the June 17, 1998 Temporary Order.

(10) I understand that expenses do not generally have an effect on support obligations, but in my situation, I have three more children at home to support.

(11) If I do not get immediate relief from this order, these children will suffer the consequences.

(12) I had a lawyer represent me at the June 17 hearing, but he forgot to mention most of what I state above. I am now representing myself.

Wherefor I respectfully request that this Honorable Court reconsider and revoke its Temporary Order of June 17, 1998.

Respectfully submitted

July 1, 1998
For Hearing August 3, 1998

Kevin Holmes, Defendant

Certificate of Service

I, Kevin Holmes, hereby swear and affirm that I have served a copy of this motion on Plaintiff Catherine Norton by sending a copy to her by first class mail, postage prepaid at her residence 39 Farm Road, Bellingham MA 02019 together with notice that a hearing has been scheduled in Dedham on the 3rd day of August, 1998 at 9 a.m.

Signed under pains and penalties of perjury this 1st day of July, 1998.

Kevin Holmes

Commonwealth of Massachusetts

The Trial Court

<u>Suffolk</u> **Division**   **Probate and Family Court Department**   **Docket No.** <u>97D-4329</u>

COMPLAINT FOR GRANDPARENT(S) VISITATION

Ada St. Pierre ,

John St. Pierre ,
Plaintiff(s)

v.

Paige Santana St. Pierre ,

Robert St. Pierre ,
Defendant(s)

1. Now comes the plaintiff(s) in this action seeking to obtain visitation rights with ~~his/her~~/their grandchild(ren), namely:

Trevor St. Pierre	12-14-92
(name of child)	(date of birth)
Travis St. Pierre	4-5-94
(name of child)	(date of birth)
Sally St. Pierre	8-12-95
(name of child)	(date of birth)
(name of child)	(date of birth)

who ~~is~~ (are) unmarried minor(s) who reside(~~s~~) at _____

21 Joy Street
_____(street address)

Boston	Suffolk County	MA	02114
(city or town)	(county)	(state)	(zip code)

and

2. Plaintiff(s) ~~is~~(are) the ~~maternal~~/paternal grandmother — ~~maternal~~/paternal grandfather — of said child(ren) who reside(~~s~~) at 39 Gray Street
_____(street address)

Boston	Suffolk County	MA	02116
(city or town)	(county)	(state)	(zip code)

3. [X] The defendant, _Paige Santana St. Pierre_
(name of defendant mother)

who resides at _21 Joy Street_
(street address)

Boston	Suffolk County	MA	02114
(city or town)	(county)	(state)	(zip code)

and the defendant, _Robert St. Pierre_
(name of defendant father)

who resides at 158 Baker Street
(street address)

San Francisco	San Francisco	CA	94117
(city or town)	(county)	(state)	(zip code)

are the parents who do not live together of the above stated child(ren).

[ ] The defendant, _____
(other, e.g., the Department of Social Services, legal guardian, etc.)

_____

_____

141

4. Please check and complete ONLY ONE of the following sections.

   a. ☐ On _____ , the defendants were divorced by judgment of the Court. The judgment did not provide for visitation rights for the above named grandparent(s).

   b. ☐ On _____ , the defendant father was adjudicated by judgment/order to be the father of the child(ren). The adjudicated father and mother of the child do not reside together. The judgment/order did not provide for visitation rights for the above named grandparent(s).

   c. ☐ On _____ , the defendants signed an acknowledgment of parentage which was approved by order/judgment of the court. The parents of the child do not reside together. The order/judgment did not provide for visitation rights for the above named grandparent(s).

   d. ☒ The defendants are married but living apart and are subject to a temporary order or judgment of separate support. The order/judgment did not provide for visitation rights for the above named grandparent(s).

   e. ☐ On _____ , _____
        (date of death)   (name of deceased parent)

        died leaving _____ as the surviving parent.
                         (name of surviving parent)

   f. ☐ On _____ , _____
        (date of death)   (name of deceased parent(1))

        died and on _____ , _____
                        (date of death)   (name of deceased parent(2))

        died. The child(ren) is/are currently _____
                                                (explain legal status of child(ren)'s care)

5. The plaintiff(s) allege(s) that it is in the best interest of the minor child(ren) that they be granted visitation with said child(ren).

   WHEREFORE plaintiff(s) request(s) that this Court enter a judgment that provides him — her — them — with visitation rights.

Date: July 2, 1998

John St. Pierre	*Ada St. Pierre*
(signature of plaintiff (2))	(signature of attorney or plaintiff(1), if pro se)
John St. Pierre	Ada St. Pierre
(PRINT name)	(PRINT name)
39 Gray Street	39 Gray Street
(Street address, if different)	(street address)
Boston MA 02116	Boston MA 02116
(city or town) (state) (zip code)	(city or town) (state) (zip code)
Tel. No. (617) 267-7597	Tel. No. (617) 267-7597

For Defendant(s):   B.B.O. # _____

Paige Santana St. Pierre   **COMPLAINT — JUDGMENT**
(name)

21 Joy Street   Filed: _____
(street address)

Boston   MA   02114   Judgment: _____
(city or town) (state) (zip code)

Tel. No. ( ) Unlisted   Temporary Orders: _____

B.B.O. # _____   Service on Summons: _____

INSTRUCTIONS

1. Refer to G.L.M. c. 119, § 39D.
2. A Care and Custody Affidavit shall be filed with this complaint. (See Page 92)
3. Service is to be made in accordance with the Rules of Domestic Relations Procedure (Rule 4).
4. No fee shall be required for the filing of this complaint.
5. If the defendant father has been ajudicated in another court copies of the judgment/order must be filed.

ADDITIONAL COPIES

pre-paid orders

$ 19.95 each, plus

4.00 per order postage

and handling to

DIVORCE HANDBOOK

P.O. Box 743

Weston MA 02493

bookstore and credit card orders

1-800-247-6553

www.bookmasters.com